CHARLES HENRY ROBINSON

HAUSALAND

OR

FIFTEEN HUNDRED MILES THROUGH

THE CENTRAL SOUDAN

Elibron Classics
www.elibron.com

Elibron Classics series.

© 2005 Adamant Media Corporation.

ISBN 1-4021-8791-2 (paperback)
ISBN 1-4212-9589-X (hardcover)

This Elibron Classics Replica Edition is an unabridged facsimile
of the edition published in 1896 by Sampson Low, Marston and Co., Ltd.,
London.

HAUSALAND

OR

FIFTEEN HUNDRED MILES THROUGH THE CENTRAL SOUDAN

✳

Charles H. Robinson

From a photograph by Clark, Cambridge

Sampson Low, Marston & Co. Ltd   F. Jenkins, Heliog, Paris

HAUSALAND

OR

FIFTEEN HUNDRED MILES THROUGH THE CENTRAL SOUDAN

BY

CHARLES HENRY ROBINSON, M.A.,

TRINITY COLLEGE, CAMBRIDGE

WITH MAP AND ILLUSTRATIONS

LONDON

SAMPSON LOW, MARSTON AND COMPANY

LIMITED

St. Dunstan's House

FETTER LANE, FLEET STREET, E.C.

1896

LONDON :

PRINTED BY WILLIAM CLOWES AND SONS, LIMITED,

STAMFORD STREET AND CHARING CROSS.

INTRODUCTION.

WITHIN the last few weeks, public interest has been specially aroused in the Hausa people by the announcement that a considerable portion of the troops selected to take part in our war with Ashanti is to consist of Hausas. Almost simultaneous with this announcement was a statement in the French papers to the effect that the French Government had decided to hold their newly acquired possessions in Madagascar with Hausa troops enlisted on the West Coast. The fact that the Hausas are so greatly in demand as soldiers might naturally suggest the conclusion that they are essentially a military race and fond of war for its own sake. As will appear, however, from the account here given, the exact opposite is in reality the case : they are a nation not of soldiers but of traders, and though they excel all the coast tribes in their power of fighting, they excel them far more in their trading and commercial enterprise. An article of mine which was printed in a recent number of the *Pall Mall Gazette*, descriptive of the town of Kano, appeared under the title of "The Manchester of Tropical Africa," a title which, as I think every reader of Chapter VIII. will admit, conveys no exaggerated idea of the importance of the town from a manufacturing and commercial point of view.

The object with which the journey here described was undertaken is explained in Chapter II. I would like to take this opportunity of expressing my most earnest gratitude to my two travelling companions, Dr. T. J. Tonkin and Mr. J. Bonner. To their unselfish and untiring exertions, often under most trying circumstances, the success of the expedition may be said to have been entirely due. I have also to thank Mr. Wm. Bidlake, of Sutton Coldfields, for help in preparing some of the illustrations, and Mr. F. E. Bennett, of Shrewsbury, and Rev. J. O. Murray, of Cambridge, the secretary of the Hausa Association, for kindly correcting the MS. of the book. For permission to use several of the photographs which appear, I am indebted to the kindness of the Earl of Scarborough and the representatives of the late Mr. Joseph Thomson.

The system of transliteration which I have adopted for representing the sound of geographical names is that originally propounded by the Royal Geographical Society, which has been sanctioned by the British Government and, with one or two unimportant modifications, by nearly all the governments of Europe.

The general principle of the system is this : the
vowels are pronounced as in Italian, the consonants
as in English, every letter is pronounced, and no
redundant letters are introduced.   Thus Ashanti
should be written, not Ashantee ; Hausa, not Haussa,
or Housa, or Haoussa, or Husa, as I have seen it
variously written.   The diphthong *au* is to be sounded
as *ow* is in the English word "how."

To those who are desirous of assisting in a practical
way the advancement of the higher interests of the
Hausa people, I would commend the perusal of
Appendix II., and more especially its concluding
paragraph.

C. H. R.

TRINITY COLLEGE, CAMBRIDGE.
January 20th, 1896.

CONTENTS.

CHAPTER I.

THE RIVER NIGER.

CHAPTER II.

THE HAUSA ASSOCIATION.

CHAPTER III.

UP THE RIVER NIGER.

CHAPTER IV.

LOKO TO KAFFI.

CHAPTER V.

KAFFI TO ZARIA.

CHAPTER VI.

ZARIA.

CHAPTER VII.

ARRIVAL AT KANO.

CHAPTER XII.

THE HAUSA LANGUAGE.

CHAPTER XIII.

MOHAMMEDANISM IN THE CENTRAL SOUDAN.

CHAPTER XIV.

THE PILGRIMAGE TO MECCA.

CHAPTER XV.

NATIVE CUSTOMS, ETC.—PREPARATION FOR LEAVING KANO.

CHAPTER XVI.

KANO TO BIRNIN-GWARI.

CHAPTER XVII.

BIRNIN-GWARI TO BIDA.

CHAPTER XVIII.

BIDA TO EGGA.

CHAPTER XIX.

EGGA TO LIVERPOOL.

CHAPTER XX.

APPENDICES.

LIST OF ILLUSTRATIONS

ILLUSTRATIONS IN TEXT

MAP.

Map of
WESTERN AFRICA
to accompany "Hausaland; or
Fifteen Hundred Miles through the Central Soudan,"
by
CHAS. H. ROBINSON, M.A.

HAUSALAND;

OR,

FIFTEEN HUNDRED MILES THROUGH THE CENTRAL SOUDAN.

———◇———

CHAPTER I.

THE RIVER NIGER.

"AFRICA," wrote a modern schoolboy, when asked to say what he knew of the Dark Continent, "is a large country chiefly composed of sand and elephants, the centre of which was uninhabited until that wicked man Stanley filled it up with towns and villages." It is of a portion of the continent which Mr. Stanley has not yet had the opportunity of filling with towns and villages, but which is none the less exceedingly well supplied with the same, that this book treats. So many travellers have crossed and recrossed Africa within the last twenty years, and so much light has, as a result, been shed even into its darkest recesses, that it seems scarcely credible that there should still remain a people so numerous as to form one per cent. of the whole population of the globe, whose country and language have remained up to the present almost completely unknown, at least to the general public. Nor can the neglect with which this people has so long been treated be justified by the fact that they were so low in the scale of civilisation, or their country so devoid of interest, that the study of them and of their surroundings might not unreasonably be postponed till the rest of the Dark Continent had been opened up. So far, indeed, is this from being the case that, in the opinion of all who have had the opportunity of instituting a comparison, the Hausas are superior, both intellectually and physically, to all other natives of equatorial Africa. Perhaps the truest explanation of the neglect above referred to is to be found in the fact that Hausaland, or the country inhabited by the Hausa people, has been, and to a large extent still is, cut off from intercourse with Europeans by two physical obstacles of more than ordinary magnitude. Hausaland proper extends, roughly speaking, from latitude 8° N. to 14° N., and from longitude 4° E. to 11° E. Of the two possible ways by which a traveller from the coast can approach this territory, the shortest and most obvious is to ascend the river Niger for about three hundred miles and then proceed overland; the distance to Kano, the most important town in the Hausa States, being about four hundred miles from it, or from the river Binué. The reason why this route has so seldom been attempted is partly, because only within the present century has the lower portion of the river Niger been explored, and partly, because of the great loss of life which has been experienced since the opening up of this route, alike by missionaries, traders, and explorers, in their efforts to penetrate the interior by ascending the river from its mouth. The other possible way is by crossing the Great Sahara from the Mediterranean coast. The distance to Kano by this route is nearly two thousand miles, by far the greater portion of which is across an almost waterless desert. Apart from the difficulties of actual travel, the European, as experience has shown, is liable to be attacked by the Tuareks who infest the desert wells, and, to a large extent, support themselves by the plunder of the caravans, which are compelled to approach them. The difficulties moreover connected with this route have been greatly aggravated by the recent occupation of Timbuctoo by the French; indeed, owing to this and other troubles in the neighbourhood of Lake Tchad, which will be alluded to later on, this route is at present closed to Europeans altogether.

Before commencing the actual narrative of our travels, it would be well to give a very brief account of the discovery of the lower waters of the river Niger, which forms the chief link of connection between Hausaland and the outside world.

Although the existence of the upper waters of this river was known upwards of two thousand years ago, it is only within the present century that its outlet into the sea has been ascertained. To anyone unacquainted with the appearance which the mouth, or rather mouths, of the Niger present from the sea, it might seem almost incredible that the outlet of so gigantic a river, which has a course of over

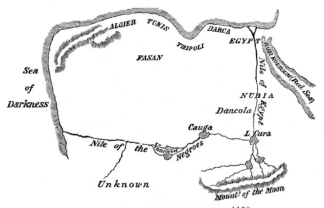

AFRICA AS KNOWN TO EDRISI, A.D. 1150.

two thousand five hundred miles, should have so long remained unknown. The explanation is to be found in the intricate network of creeks extending for two hundred miles or more along the coast, through which the river, divided and subdivided into a large number of streams, no one of which is sufficiently big to attract any special attention, creeps unnoticed into the sea. The upper Niger seems clearly to be referred to by Herodotus * B.C. 450, when he is recounting a tale which he had heard in Egypt, of five young Nasamones, who, setting out from the country to the south-west of Egypt, had after a thirsty journey over a sandy desert, reached a land of pygmies watered by lakes and marshes, abounding with fruit-trees, and through which ran from west to east a great river. The Roman historian Pliny, A.D. 80, refers to the Niger, and states that it flows into the Nile. The Arabian Edrisi, A.D. 1150, asserts that the Niger flows from, not to, the sources of the Nile. The great African traveller and historian Leo Africanus, A.D. 1520, believed that it rose in a lake south of Bornou and eventually flowed into the Atlantic. To come down to still more recent time, the African Association, which was afterwards incorporated with the Royal Geographical Society, sent out in 1788 a man named T. Ledyard with instructions to go *viâ* Cairo to search for the Niger. In 1795 the same Association sent out Mungo Park, who went up the Gambia, and reaching the Niger found it flowing from west to east. Having returned to England in 1799, after successfully exploring three hundred miles of the middle Niger, he was sent out again by the Government in 1804, but after adding considerably to his former discoveries, he was at

* Herodotus ii. 32.

length drowned at Busa on the middle Niger. In 1816, an expedition proceeded up the Congo in the hope of reaching the Niger, but after going two hundred and eighty miles they were forced to retire without having satisfied themselves as to the identity or otherwise of the two rivers. In 1826, Clapperton, who had previously heard of the Niger whilst staying

ROCK AT BUSA, SCENE OF MUNGO PARK'S DEATH.

in Sokoto, which he had reached by crossing the Great Sahara, was despatched by the Government from the west coast together with two naval officers and a servant named Lander. On the death of his three companions, Lander, who had already reached Busa on the Niger, returned to the coast, to be again despatched on the same quest in 1830. On this occasion, after reaching Busa, he succeeded in de-

scending the Niger in a native canoe to the sea, thus
solving the problem which for centuries, and even
decades of centuries, had remained insoluble.

As the result of the enthusiasm created by this
discovery, an Association was formed, of which Mr.
Macgregor Laird was the leading spirit, with the object
of establishing trade relations with the people of the
interior. The first expedition despatched by the
Association was a disastrous failure, forty out of forty-
nine Europeans dying on the river. Nothing daunted
by the fate of his predecessors, Consul Beecroft, in
1840, succeeded in pushing up the river in a small
steamer as far as Rabba, a distance of about five
hundred miles. In the following year a carefully
prepared expedition, consisting of three steamers,
was sent out by the Government, with the view of
forming some permanent settlement on the river.
Forty-one out of a hundred and fifty-five Europeans
having died of fever within two months, the idea of
such a settlement was for the moment abandoned as
impracticable ; but a further expedition, organised
once more by Mr. Laird in 1854, having ascended the
Binué for some considerable distance and without any
serious sickness amongst the crew, led to the establishment of one or two trading-stations on the Niger
and to the appointment of a British Consular Agent
at Lokoja, the confluence of the Niger and the Binué.
The subsequent withdrawal of this officer and of the

Parliamentary grant for opening up the Niger, the death of Mr. Laird, and the destruction of his station by the natives, caused the abandonment for a time of European enterprise there. After some years, a few firms gradually recommenced operations, and in 1879 amalgamated into a single private company. In 1880 the French appeared upon the scene, which led to the formation of a large public British company for the purpose of buying up all interests in the Niger, obtaining treaties with the native rulers, and procuring a charter from Great Britain similar to that formerly held by the East India Company. A keen struggle ensued between the French and their English rivals, which ended in 1884, when the French sold all their existing property to the English Niger Company. Two years later, in 1886, the Company, having made about three hundred treaties with natives, states, and tribes, including the whole of the Hausa States, received from the Crown its present charter, and assumed the title, by which it is now known, of Royal Niger Company. Governing rights over the whole of this immense region were by the charter entrusted to the Company, to whom the credit of having secured to England one of her most valuable possessions in Africa is entirely due. In order to appreciate the national service thus rendered by the Company, it is necessary to recall how very nearly the sovereignty of this region was

lost, first to France and afterwards to Germany.
The settlement of two French companies on the
lower Niger, which was effected in 1880 under
the influence of Gambetta, was intended as a step
towards the realisation of the dream of a vast
African empire extending from the Mediterranean
to the Congo. This dream was for ever dispelled
by the commercial victory gained by the Company
in 1884, as the result of which the French flag
disappeared altogether from the lower Niger. But
no sooner had the Company got rid of the French
claims than they were called upon to deal with
a still more formidable rival. In April, 1885,
Herr Flegel left Berlin, under the auspices of the
German African Society and the German Colonial
Society, with instructions to ascend the lower Niger
and to endeavour to make treaties with the Sultans
of Sokoto and Gando with the object of securing to
Germany the whole of the Hausa States, communication with which would, it was hoped, eventually be
opened up from the hinterland of the German
Cameroons. Most fortunately, in view of the future
development of English interests on the river, the
English Company had as its guiding spirit a man
endowed with more than average foresight and
energy in the person of Sir George Taubman Goldie.
Having ascertained beforehand the intentions of the
Germans, he succeeded in despatching Mr. Joseph

Thomson, who had just returned from Masailand, some two months in advance of Herr Flegel, in order to secure for the Company, and thus for England, treaties with the above-mentioned sultans, the effect of which would be to bring within the English sphere of influence the whole of the territories subject to their sway. As Mr. Thomson was returning with these treaties duly signed, he met Herr Flegel proceeding up the river on a fruitless errand.

By the terms of the charter, by which something like half a million square miles were placed under their jurisdiction, the Royal Niger Company are authorised to levy dues on all trade on the lower Niger and Binué, the amount so raised to be spent by the Company on administrative purposes. In order to collect these dues and to enforce its prohibition of spirits and modern firearms above latitude 7° N., the Company has found it necessary to place guardships at certain points in order to prevent goods being smuggled into the river, whether by Europeans or natives. The restrictions thus placed upon what can only be described as illegitimate trade have led to an intensely bitter feeling between the native traders of Brass and the officials of the Company, which culminated in an attack upon Akassa in January 1895 and in a massacre of about sixty of the native agents of the Company. It is earnestly to be hoped that one result of this lamentable occurrence will be the prohibition of the importation of gunpowder and fire-arms throughout the Niger Coast Protectorate, which is a sort of Crown colony and governed directly from England.

As stated above, the Royal Niger Company have placed an absolute prohibition upon the importation of spirits and modern firearms above latitude 7°N., *i.e.*, above the actual delta of the Niger, a restriction which is so far effective that, in the course of a journey of over a thousand miles through the Hausa States, I do not remember seeing a single bottle of spirits or more than half-a-dozen rifles.

CHAPTER II.

THE HAUSA ASSOCIATION.

On the 26th of June, 1891, there died at Lokoja, on the river Niger, John Alfred Robinson M.A., a scholar of Christ's College, Cambridge, who was one of the first Englishmen to realise the importance of studying the Hausa language, and who had himself acquired a considerable knowledge of it by living in familiar contact with the Hausas themselves, a large number of whom are to be found at Lokoja. A few months later a small but representative gathering took place at the Charing Cross Hotel, at which it was decided that an attempt should be made to perpetuate the memory and to carry on the work of Mr. J. A. Robinson by "providing for a thoroughly scientific study of the Hausa language with a view of promoting the higher interests of that people and of translating the Scriptures and other appropriate literature into their tongue." * Mr. J. A. Robinson had been working in connection with the Church Missionary Society, but the founders of the Hausa Association determined, in accordance with the wide

* For further account of " Hausa Association " *cf.* Appendix II.

G. WILMOT BROOKE AND JOHN ALFRED ROBINSON IN HAUSA DRESS.

[To face page 13.

sympathies which he had been known to entertain, to endeavour to enlist the support of all who would be likely to take an interest in the welfare of this great people, whether from a missionary, a scientific, or a commercial standpoint. The varied interests represented on the committee of the Association may be seen from the fact that it included the names of six Archbishops and Bishops, in addition to several others specially interested in missionary work; of four distinguished philologists, viz., Professors Max Müller, Peile, Margoliouth and Robertson Smith; of two specially interested in science, viz., Francis Galton, F.R.S., and Major Darwin; and, lastly, of three representatives of West African enterprise, the late Lord Aberdare Governor of the Royal Niger Company, Sir George Taubman Goldie then deputy governor, and the late Mr. Macgregor Laird a descendant of one of the earliest pioneers alike of trade and discovery on the Niger. In order to secure the carrying out of the objects of the Association, the executive committee decided to appoint one or more " students," who should proceed at once to the Hausa States for the purpose of studying the language and customs of the people on the spot. In accordance with this decision, advertisements were inserted in leading scientific, literary, and religious periodicals extending over some twelve months, in answer to which a considerable number

of applications for the post of "student" were
received, none of which however the committee found
themselves able to accept. On November 5, 1892,
whilst engaged in work at Truro, I was not a little
surprised to receive a letter from a member of the
committee, stating that at their last meeting they
had decided to ask if I would allow my name to be
submitted to them as a candidate for the Hausa
studentship. After full consideration, it seemed
wrong to refuse the opportunity thus offered of
carrying on my brother's work, and as the result of
a personal interview with the committee it was
arranged that I should place myself at the disposal
of the Association from the following April. The
instructions which I received from my committee
were to proceed with as little delay as possible to
Kano and to other large towns in the Hausa States,
where the Hausa language might be studied to the
greatest advantage. As, however, it was supposed
that the climate throughout a large portion of
Hausaland was such as to render doubtful the
possibility of any lengthened stay, it was thought
better that a preliminary study both of Hausa and
Arabic should be make either in Tripoli or Tunis
before proceeding into the far interior. In accordance therefore with such instructions, I left England
on April 30, 1893, reaching Tripoli about a fortnight later. The two objects which I had in

view on landing were, first to continue my study of the Hausa and Arabic languages, and secondly to obtain information as to the possibility of crossing the Great Sahara from Tripoli and of thus avoiding the long tract of unhealthy country which separates the greater part of Hausaland from the Niger.

The town of Tripoli contains a population of thirty thousand, about six or seven hundred of whom speak the Hausa language. The greater part of these have come across the desert as slaves or servants, and, though most of them can speak two or more languages, they are quite uneducated and illiterate. There are however a certain number of educated natives, called by the Hausas " Mallams," from an Arabic word meaning to teach, who are to be found from time to time *en route* as pilgrims to or from Mecca. It is no uncommon occurrence for as many as a thousand pilgrims from the interior to embark at Tripoli in a single day. The account given me by one such, a man who acted as my teacher during my stay in

HAUSA PILGRIM TO MECCA.

Tripoli, of his journey from Hausaland to Mecca, affords a typical example of the difficulties connected with the pilgrimage. He had started originally from Bida, a town about a hundred miles north of the junction of the rivers Niger and Binué, distant as the bird flies two hundred miles from Mecca, and had taken with him his wives and family, a party of seventeen in all. They travelled in the first instance to Kano and thence to Kuka, the capital of Bornou, situated near to the western shore of Lake Tchad. The king being absent on a slave raid, he was detained here for some four months, after which he made his way into Wadai and thence to Darfur, in which latter province he and his party were seized as slaves and retained as such for a year. At the end of this time, having succeeded in regaining his liberty and that of his family, on the plea that being pilgrims *en route* for Mecca they could not lawfully be detained, he proceeded in safety as far as the Mahdi's camp at Omdurman, where he arrived just after the fall of Khartoum and the death of General Gordon. The account which he dictated to me in Hausa of the capture of Khartoum differed chiefly from other accounts in the emphasis which he laid upon the resistance which the Mahdi met with in the final attack upon the city. After a month's delay at Ondurman, and having with difficulty escaped from the hands of the Mahdi, who

wished to retain him as a soldier, he made his way
into Abyssinia. Here he got into trouble again, the
result being that a whole year elapsed before he and
his party succeeded in reaching the coast at Souakim,
whence they travelled by steamer to Jeddah, the
port of Mecca. After duly performing the rites of
the pilgrimage both at Mecca and Medina, he was
prevented from resuming his homeward journey
owing to the entire exhaustion of his resources.
According to his account, it is customary for any
pilgrim, who has money wherewith to do so, to
entertain his fellow pilgrims at a banquet given in
their honour, and, as there are sometimes as many as
sixty thousand pilgrims to be found at a time in
Mecca, it will easily be seen what unlimited opportunities for getting rid of money are here afforded.
Having spent all that he possessed, he and his friends
were forced to remain in Mecca for no less than four
years, at the end of which time, having recruited their
resources from those of the pilgrims who had come
after him, they returned to Jeddah and, sailing thence
to Suez, walked across Egypt to Alexandria, whence
they came on by sea to Tripoli. The last that I
heard of him was that he was about to start across
the Great Sahara desert and that he hoped to reach
his own town in about a year's time. As he had not
apparently arrived at Bida at the time of my recent
visit to it, it is to be feared that some further mis-

fortunes have befallen him by the way. Should he succeed in reaching his destination within the year 1895 he will then have travelled a distance of nearly seven thousand miles, the time occupied being rather over ten years. From travellers such as these it is possible to gain a very fair knowledge of colloquial Hausa, and at the same time to collect a good deal of interesting information in regard to travelling in the far interior. After a stay of rather less than three months in Tripoli, it became evident that it would be impossible even to attempt the crossing of the desert from thence.

The province of Tripoli is under Turkish rule, and the Pasha professes to have received strict orders from Constantinople to prevent any European traveller from going more than ten miles into the interior, the alleged reason being that any such would be almost certainly murdered by the tribes who live to the south of the province of Tripoli.

It was suggested to me that this difficulty might be overcome by obtaining, through the intervention of the British Ambassador at Constantinople, a firman, the effect of which would be to override any local opposition. Previous experience however of the value to be attached to Turkish firmans convinced me of the inutility of adopting such a suggestion. When about to travel through Cilicia and part of Armenia in 1892, I applied to Constantinople for a

firman to enable me, as I hoped, to overcome the
difficulties which are always thrown in the way of
Englishmen who attempt to mix with Armenians in
their own country. As a preliminary to the granting
of the firman, I was asked to send in a list of the
various places which I proposed to visit. This
having been done, it was granted in due form, but
was purposely forwarded too late to overtake me;
and, as I eventually learnt prior to leaving the
country, a telegram was sent from headquarters to
the governor of each place mentioned in the firman
warning him that an Englishman was coming, and
requesting him to place every obstacle in the way of
my further progress. Had I obtained a firman for
travelling in the interior of the province of Tripoli,
seeret orders of a similar character would undoubtedly
have been sent to the governor of Murzouk, the first
important place to the south of the town of Tripoli,
which no bribe, that I could have afforded, would
have induced him to disobey, and which would have
led to my compulsory return to the coast. Having
satisfied myself as to the impossibility of reaching
the Hausa States from Tripoli, I left that place for
Tunis in order to ascertain whether a start could be
made from there. Landing at Gabes with Mr. H.
Harris, who had been my host at Tripoli, we bought
a couple of camels and proceeded to make an
excursion of about three weeks across a piece of the

desert which lies to the south of Tunis and Algiers. The following brief extracts from a diary kept on this journey will give some idea of the nature of the country traversed :—

June 10.—Pitched our tents at an oasis which has been formed by an artesian well constructed by M. Lesseps, the water from which rises twenty-five feet into the air, and is made to irrigate four or five hundred acres of land, on which are grown date-palms, pomegranates, tomatoes, onions, and cucumbers. Previous to the construction of this well, the whole of this oasis was nothing but barren sand.

June 13.—Our thermometer to-day registered $107\frac{1}{2}°$ in the shade. Soon after starting, we encountered a burning sirocco wind driving fine sand before it; the worst of it passed in about an hour and a half. At 6.30 we halted for the night, having failed to come across any well, and having therefore to depend upon the water which we had brought with us in skins. The water carried in these skins, which, when put in at the well, is usually gray, is of a dark-brown colour when served out for drinking.

June 23. — Reached Feriana this morning at 7.30 A.M. About half a mile outside the place are the remains of the old Roman town, extending for upwards of a mile; four pillars of a temple, and the ruins of a large number of other buildings, are still

RUINS OF CHRISTIAN CHURCH AT TEBESSA.

[To face page 21.

visible ; no water at present exists on the site of the old city.

June 24.—Started last night at 9.0 to ride through the night in order to avoid the heat of the day. Riding a camel by moonlight is a most strange sensation ; the camel looks nearly twice as large as in daylight, and the solemnity of the animal harmonises most curiously with the natural feeling of solemnity which the clear midnight sky produces. During the night we crossed a pass in the Atlas Mountains, the height according to the aneroid being 4600 feet.

June 26.—Visited Roman ruins at Tebessa, consisting of a prætorium built in the first century, and converted into a Christian church in the fourth ; a temple of Minerva ; an arch of the time of Caracalla ; a bath, the mosaic of which is in a wonderful state of preservation ; and many other public and private buildings.

June 29.—Reached Tunis by train from Tebessa, distant about two hundred miles ; after sleeping on the ground for three weeks with innumerable insects crawling over one, the luxury of a bed is indescribable.

A few days later I returned for a time to England, in order to spend a few months in the study of medicine, and to be present at some meetings organised

by friends of the Hausa Association.   Later on I
returned again to Tunis, together with Dr. T. J.
Tonkin, who had arranged to accompany me on my
journey to Kano, and who was desirous of gaining
some knowledge of colloquial Hausa previous to

T. J. TONKIN, M.R.C.S. EDIN., L.R.C.P.
[*Photo. by A. King, Littlehampton.*]

starting.   On this occasion we remained for six
months, occupying ourselves almost exclusively with
the study of Hausa and Arabic, though at the same
time making all possible inquiries as to the feasibility
of getting into the Sahara from here.   There are in

all about a thousand natives, from countries south of the Great Desert, to be found in Tunis, though a considerable number of these do not speak Hausa, Bornuese being at least equally spoken. They are subject to a so-called king of the negroes, who is a retired slave-dealer and has been appointed by them as their sheik, and to whom they all pay tribute.

The province of Tunis is to all intents a French possession, the power of the Bey having been completely broken and being now merely nominal. Since their occupation, the French have made repeated efforts to get into touch with the Tuarek and other tribes who live in the northern part of the Sahara, their great desire being to divert the trade from the Hausa and Bornu countries, which now goes to Tripoli, to either Gabes or Tunis. They have even proposed to run a railway right across the desert to Lake Tchad, in order to secure for themselves not only the trade which at present finds its outlet at Tripoli, but a portion at least of that which goes southwards to the Niger. Various preliminary surveys have already been made, and it has been suggested that the railway should start from the south of Algeria and have three southern termini, one at St. Louis, another at Timbuctoo, and a third at Lake Tchad. The difficulties connected with running a railway for two thousand miles across an almost waterless desert, though not actually insuper-

able, are such as to make any company, or even
nation, hesitate long before finally committing
themselves to so heroic an undertaking. The
probable cost of such a railway would be twenty
millions sterling, and, though it might in course of
time be the means of increasing the native demand
for European goods, many generations would probably
elapse before it would pay its own working expenses,
i.e., including the necessary military defences at the
various desert stations, to say nothing of any interest
on the original capital.

Another still more romantic proposal was made by
the late M. Lesseps, to render fertile a considerable
tract of what is now desert by letting in the water of
the Mediterranean by means of a canal. A more
accurate survey of the land in the province of Tunis,
which it was proposed to flood, and which was
believed to be considerably below the level of the
sea, has shown that the level of most of the ground
is so little below that of the sea that the final result
of letting it in would be to cover the soil with a deep
layer of salt, which would be left after the evapora-
tion of the water. If the desert is ever to be in any
way reclaimed, and if a route available for Europeans
is to be opened to Lake Tchad and the Hausa States,
it will only be by sinking a series of artesian wells,
an experiment which, as stated above, has already
been tried with partial success. At the present

moment no trade of any value comes either to Tunis
or Algiers from the countries south of the Sahara, and
it is very doubtful whether the French will ever
succeed in getting into their hands the existing trade
to Tripoli, without first gaining actual possession of
that province.

The longer we remained in Tunis, the more obvious

MR. JOHN BONNER.
[*Photo. by A. Holborn, Bristol.*]

it became that it would be impossible to start thence
for any expedition across the Sahara, even if, as
seemed by no means likely, the French authorities in
Tunis could be induced to give their approval to such
an attempt. Since the massacre of the Flatters
expedition in 1881, they have themselves abstained
from sending any further expeditions into the heart

of the desert, and, as the hostility of the Tuareks has increased rather than decreased since that time, owing to the occupation of Timbuctoo, it would be, to say the least, extremely hazardous for any European to attempt to cross it.

Having continued therefore our study of Hausa and Arabic for six months, we left Tunis again, in June, 1894, in order to complete our final preparations in England, prior to starting for Hausaland by way of the Niger.

Just before leaving Tunis, I accepted an offer from Mr. John Bonner, who had gained a very fair knowledge of colloquial Arabic, as the result of two years' residence in Tripoli, to accompany our expedition, to the success of which he contributed in a very marked degree.

CHAPTER III

UP THE RIVER NIGER.

DURING our brief stay in England, two meetings were held on behalf of the Hausa Association; the first on July 3rd in the London Chamber of Commerce, presided over by Sir A. Rollit, M.P., at which Mr. H. H. Johnston and Mr. H. M. Stanley contributed some personal reminiscences of their intercourse with Hausa natives. Mr. Johnston said: "In the course of my African travels I have been struck by the greater spread of the Hausa people as travellers, and of their language, than of any other race in the northern part of Africa. That nation which is to acquire the greatest control over the Central Soudan, the greatest influence in politics and trade, must first of all acquire a supreme influence over the Hausa people. In Africa there are four great languages of the present and the future—English, Arabic, Hausa and Swahili. If we can obtain a mastery over the last three, we shall enter more readily into the minds and views of the people of Africa; inasmuch as in the north of Africa Arabic

will suffice, to the south of the northern portion
Hausa, and south of that again Swahili.　I sincerely
hope some day to see chairs founded in our great
universities for the study of Hausa and Swahili.　If
we intend to be the dominant power in Africa we
must certainly take up very earnestly the study of
those two languages."

Mr. Stanley spoke of the Hausas whom he had met
on the Congo, and contrasted the Hausas' love of
books with the superstitious dread of the same
exhibited by the illiterate pagan tribes of the Congo.

The second meeting was held on July 13th in the
Liverpool Town Hall under the presidency of the
Lord Mayor, at which Sir George Taubman Goldie
and others spoke.　On the following morning Dr.
Tonkin, Mr. Bonner, Salam, an Arab servant whom
I had brought with me from Tunis, and I, embarked
on board the s.s. *Loanda*, which was bound for
Akassa at the mouth of the river Niger.　The follow-
ing are extracts from a diary kept on the voyage :—

July 21.—Landed at Sierra Leone ; interesting
talk with the acting Governor of the colony, who had
recently returned from a six-hundred-mile walk in
the interior.　The accounts which he gave of the
slave trade at the back of the colony were most
discouraging ; until quite recently slave-raiding had
been going on within four days' march of Freetown ;
farther inland he had passed for seven days at a time

through burnt villages and country which had been desolated by the Sofas' slave ravages. In one place he came across a heap of bodies of slaves who had just been killed, their owners having heard of his approach. He is taking the most active measures to put a stop to this state of things for the future.

August 1.—Passing the Liberian coast. This colony, which was started in 1822, consists of twenty thousand native emigrants from North America and their descendants. The state of things at present existing in Liberia may well be an answer to those who think that the west African native is, or can within any given space of time be rendered, capable of governing himself. As no one will consent to pay any taxes, the public revenue consists entirely of import and export duties, the whole amount so raised being divided up amongst the Government officials, and nothing being ever spent on public works or improvements of any kind. The only point in which the Liberians excel, perhaps, all the other inhabitants of the globe, is in their amazing self-conceit. Their army, I was informed, consists of 1000 men, 998 of whom regard themselves as officers. When some French warships recently called, the Liberians gravely assured the commander that, during the next European war, they had decided to remain neutral! From a European standpoint the adminis-tration of justice is more original than satisfactory.

A native judge having recently given a decision against a certain litigant, the latter held up his revolver in court and said: "I guess and calculate, Mr. Judge, that unless you think differently, I shall send one of these bullets through you," whereupon the decision was promptly reversed. As an attempt at native colonisation and self-government, the history of Liberia would indeed be a most entertaining farce, were it not also a most significant tragedy.

August 5.—Reached Accra, where we were most hospitably entertained by the Governor, Sir Brandford Griffith. There are about five hundred Hausa troops stationed here, several of whom, together with one of their Mallams, came to see Dr. Tonkin and myself. They seemed greatly pleased at being able to talk to a European in their own language. I gave the Mallam one of the copies of St. Matthew's gospel, which I had had lithographed in Tunis, which he will, I think, read carefully. The Governor says that, in order to encourage English officials to learn a native language, a bonus of £50 is paid to anyone who does so; Hausa is the language most frequently attempted. It appears that the natives here have a great objection to a census of their villages being taken, for fear lest this should be a preliminary to taxation. The difficulty in the case of certain villages was overcome by the expedient of sending up a band; as everyone without exception turned out to hear the music, all that had then to be done was to count the auditors. The English language in a most mutilated form is spoken by the natives, and English money passes, though coins of an earlier date than the present reign are refused. A native returned a shilling stamped with the head of George IV. with the remark, " Queen Victoria, he be King now!"

August 16.—Anchored inside the Forcados river, which is in reality one of the mouths of the Niger, in order to unload cargo into the branch steamer for Lagos.

The river Niger, as has been already stated, finds its way into the sea by a large number of different mouths, of which those at Forcados and Akassa are the most important. On leaving Forcados, our steamer proceeded up the Benin creek, which was at times upwards of a mile in width and again so narrow that the ship's bow touched the trees on the bank in turning round the corners. The banks on either side of the innumerable creeks, of which the delta is composed, are covered with mangroves, the mangrove being a spreading tree from ten to forty feet high, growing by preference in liquid mud in which it would be impossible for a man to walk. The mangrove swamp extends itself by the several trees dropping hanging roots, sometimes twenty feet

long, from their boughs; these eventually touch the
water or mud and become regular roots from which
new trees or branches arise.　A sickly odour is given
off by these swamps, the general appearance of which
is as uninteresting and monotonous as can well be
imagined.　After going some thirty miles up the
Benin creek, we anchored in sight of about half-a-
dozen English oil factories, the inhabitants of which
are unable to walk more than a few yards in any
direction, and should they wish to visit each other,
can only do so by boat.　The oil, which is taken on
board by the steamers at these factories, is used in
England as train oil and in the manufacture of soap
and candles; it is obtained from a palm which grows
amidst the mangrove swamps, the value of the
annual export from the delta being about half a
million sterling.　The whole of this delta forms what
is called "The Niger Coast Protectorate," the government of which is entrusted to a Consul-General, who
has under him a large staff of assistants.　On leaving
the neighbourhood of Benin, we sailed up another
creek to Warri, near which I noticed a native grave,
a sort of miniature hut made of sticks, on the top of
which was placed a gin bottle.　The sight of this
significant memorial made one wonder whether the
benefits, which the European is supposed to have
conferred upon the African, are in any way equal to
the harm which he has done to him by the introduc-

tion of gin and firearms. One of the government officials at Warri, however, seemed to take a more optimistic view of the situation; after detailing to me some of the horrible villainies which English and other traders had committed here prior to the establishment of the "Protectorate" in 1891, he said that he thought it was well that there were such evils in the world, as it would be so dreadfully slow and dull if everybody were good.

On Saturday, August 18, we arrived at Akassa, the first station in the territory of the Royal Niger Company, and on the following Monday we started in the s.s. *Croft*, a vessel of a thousand tons burden, to ascend the river Niger. The *Croft* took up the river, in addition to other cargo, 1600 bags of salt, *i.e.*, about eighty tons weight, salt being one of the chief media of exchange on the river, 1 cwt. of salt selling for about twelve shillings. For the first thirty miles after leaving Akassa we passed nothing but the interminable mangroves; then the soil became somewhat harder and native huts began to appear, also plantations of palm-trees, bananas, and sugar-canes; farther on we passed at intervals of about a mile native villages, consisting of from three to fifty huts, the inhabitants of which seemed all to turn out to gaze at the steamer as it went by. After steaming for two days we reached Abutshi, where the appearance of the country begins unmistakably to

D

improve.   It was an indescribable relief to the eye
to see rising ground once more after the monotonous
swamps of the delta.   On the rising ground behind
Abutshi are some coffee plantations, the growing of
coffee, which promises to be a success from a commercial point of view, having been introduced by the
Company four or five years ago.   At Abutshi, Bishop
Tugwell, in whose diocese the Niger territories lie,
came on board and travelled with us as far as Lokoja.
Leaving Abutshi on August 23rd, we passed an hour
or two later Asaba, which is the headquarters and
centre of administration of the Royal Niger Company ; at this point the river is about three-quarters
of a mile in width, its main channel, to which the
steamers have to adhere, being however comparatively narrow and zigzagging constantly from side
to side.   On August 25, five days after leaving
Akassa, we arrived at Lokoja, the situation and
general appearance of which is really very fine.   We
saw here for the first time the geological formation
with which we were afterwards to become so familiar
in the interior, and which forms so curious and
distinctive a feature of African scenery, viz., the flat-
topped table mountain.   The one at the foot of
which Lokoja lies, is 1375 feet above sea-level, and
1100 feet above Lokoja itself.

To the friends and supporters of the Hausa Association, Lokoja will always have a very special

NATIVE HOUSE AT LOKOJA, ENTRANCE TO MISSION COMPOUND.

[To face page 34.

interest as having been the spot where Mr. J. A. Robinson, in memory of whom the Association was formed, first came into contact with any considerable number of the Hausa people, and where, after acquiring a knowledge of their language by living and working amongst them, he commenced to translate the New Testament for their use. In the church at Lokoja there is a simple inscription recording his name and the name of his fellow-worker, Mr. Wilmot Brooke, who died at the same place six months later. It concludes with the words, "Except a corn of wheat fall into the ground and die, it abideth alone, but if it die it bringeth forth much fruit." It may well prove—in accordance with the Japanese proverb, "Defeat is the path to victory"—that his grave marks the first stage in the realisation of the final victory of Christianity over both the heathenism and Mohammedanism of the Central Soudan.

The situation of Lokoja, at the junction of the Niger and the Binué, renders it a place of considerable importance from a trading point of view. Small steamers run from here to Rabbah on the Niger, and to Yola on the Binué, the former distant about 200, the latter about 500 miles. On reaching this point the traveller begins to realise that a change has taken place in the outward appearance of the natives proportionate to, and to some extent connected with, the change in the character of the scenery. The tribes which inhabit the delta and the banks of the Niger below Lokoja are some of the lowest and most degraded savages that are to be found in the world. Cannibalism and human sacrifices, except in so far as the Royal Niger Company has been able to make its influence felt, are still of frequent occurrence. Even Christianity, though it has succeeded in civilising the still more degraded savages of Terra del Fuego, has as yet made but little progress here. On reaching Lokoja, however, a change is at once apparent. Even before he lands the traveller cannot but be struck by the improvement alike in the dress and in the general look of intelligence in many who gather to greet the arrival of his steamer. Nor is the favourable impression in any way diminished as he leaves the riverside and penetrates into the town. If fortunate enough to be able to speak any of the native languages of the place, he will soon come to realise, as he talks with some of the best educated and most intelligent of the inhabitants, that there is at least as great a difference between an educated and cultured Hausa, for example, and the savages whom he has left behind in the delta, as there is between the Hausa and himself.

One curious superstition * which we heard of as existing amongst several of the tribes inhabiting the banks of the Niger between this and the delta, is a

* *Cf.* Appendix III. on "Totemism."

belief in the possibility of a man possessing an *alter ego* in the form of some animal such as a crocodile or hippopotamus. It is believed that such a person's life is bound up with that of the animal to such an extent that, whatever affects the one produces a corresponding impression upon the other, and that if one dies the other must speedily do so too. It happened not very long ago that an Englishman shot a hippopotamus close to a native village ; the friends of a woman who died the same night in the village demanded and eventually obtained five pounds as compensation for the murder of the woman.

August 28.—Went yesterday to see Mr. King, a native agent of the Royal Niger Company, who says that it will be quite impossible for us to start from Loko for another two months owing to the fact that the rainy season is still on ; to wait this time, however, is quite out of the question.

The teaching of the English language to native mission agents is productive at times of somewhat ludicrous results. A native wrote thus to an English missionary at Lagos, apologising for not coming to see him : " Had not distance preponderated I should have approximated to see you." The only instance to beat this that I have heard, was a letter written by a native of India to our English representative at Zanzibar, which began with the words, " Honoured Enormity."

August 30.—Abbega the Hausa slave, who was
set free by Overweg, and who afterwards accompanied
Dr. Barth (1852–55) across the Sahara on his return
to Tripoli, and later on spent several years with
Dr. Schön in England, came up to see me. He is a
vigorous and intelligent old man, though as far as
his religion is concerned he affords but another
illustration of the uselessness of attempting to
Christianise Africans by taking them to England.
Though baptised there as a Christian he now
professes himself a Mohammedan.   At 4.30 this
afternoon I went down to endeavour to hire carriers.
Mr. King had got a large collection of Yorubas and
Nupés in his courtyard who had expressed their
willingness to be hired. It is necessary, so we are
told, to take these in preference to Hausas, as the
latter have a most awkward habit of running away
with their loads as soon as they find themselves in
their own country, whereas the others, being strangers
to the country, are supposed to be much more
reliable. I began by taking a photograph of the
set; this done I haggled for nearly two hours as to
the price I was to pay, the agreement finally come
to being that each porter should receive seven bags
of salt for the journey through to Zaria in addition
to subsistence money. The Yorubas are of a deep
chocolate colour, not nearly so dark as the Hausas.
Most of them have got one or more of their front

teeth removed, and others have some of them filed to a point. They are a fine-looking set of men and laugh energetically on very slight provocation.

September 5.—Met Captain Lugard, who has just arrived from Akassa and is on his way up the river to Borgu; he is taking with him an English doctor and an escort of forty Hausa soldiers.

September 7.—Heard this morning that half my carriers have deserted. Bonner and Salam both down with fever.

September 11.—Completed yesterday our final preparations in view of starting to-day. Mr. King had succeeded in supplying the places of my deserters. About 7.15 A.M. our motley crew of carriers appeared and immediately commenced to feel the loads one after the other in order to discover the lightest. One man picked up a gun case weighing only twenty pounds, which was intended to serve as the complement to another load, and began to march off in triumph therewith. We proceeded in a long file to the quay, but before our carriers would embark they insisted on going to bid a final farewell to their friends in the town. Many of them it appeared owed debts, and their creditors had begun to show considerable interest in their proposed travels. It is customary to give one bag of salt to each man prior to his departure, but to prevent the men taking the salt and then failing to start we had fifty

vouchers made out and handed one to each porter as
he set foot on the steamer. This he was free to hand
to his creditors or friends as he stepped on board in
order to console them for his absence. A large
crowd of people, interested from various motives in
our departure, gathered to see us start. The final
farewells occupied about three hours. The steam-

NATIVE VILLAGE ON RIVER BINUÉ.

launch which was to take us to Loko was so diminutive that when the whole of our party, including a
horse which I had bought at Lokoja, were on board,
it was so full that the only way by which the captain
could get from one end of his vessel to the other
was by climbing along outside the bulwarks.

September 12.—Anchored last night at 7.30 at a
point where the Binué is nearly a mile wide; it is

now in flood, but even in the dry season it has a width
of over half a mile. Passed some most picturesque
villages situated on the river bank to-day. Reached
Amurgedde, a station of the Royal Niger Company,
at 8.30 P.M., where we anchored for the night.

September 13.—Arrived at Loko this morning ;
sent messenger on shore to carry our greetings to the
king. He sent us return greetings and assigned us a
residence in his village. On landing I found the
king waiting for us under a tree. He conducted us
to a courtyard with a number of round conical-roofed
huts, three of which he set apart for our use. About
half an hour after our packages were all in, his
Majesty, who had previously retired, sent a message
to say that he was at home, whereupon Dr. T.
and I proceeded to pay him an official visit. He
addressed us chiefly through one of his courtiers, who
had not, however, to act as interpreter, as we all
spoke Hausa. After the reiteration of mutual salutations for the space of about ten minutes we rose to
go ; as we left the royal residence, which was a
round mud hut, much the same as those assigned to
us, there followed us, as a present, a sheep and two
loads of yams. On reaching our huts we despatched
in return a present of proportionate value.

CHAPTER IV.

LOKO TO KAFFI.

On leaving the village of Loko, our immediate destination was Zaria, a large town containing a population of about 30,000, situated some 260 miles almost due north of Loko. Marching in Central Africa is very much the same from one day to another; a description, therefore, of the incidents which occurred during the first two days will afford a very fair idea of our whole journey.

September 14.—Hoped to have got started about 6 A.M. this morning. We got up ourselves at 4.40 and before 6 were ready to set out. Then began a series of disputes, altercations and wrangles, one result of which was the discovery that we had fifty-one loads, but only fifty carriers. I accordingly decided to put one load on our horse and start thus; however, no sooner was this arrangement completed than we were informed by the natives of Loko that there was so much water lying across our route that no horse could possibly carry a load; I was there-fore reduced to the necessity of trying to find an additional carrier in Loko to go with us, at any rate as far as Nassarawa. A man having been found in the village, I agreed to pay him the price which he himself proposed, which certainly seemed far from exorbitant, viz., ten thousand cowries, or in English money five shillings, for carrying a load weighing ninety-five pounds during a four days' march. Finally, after further delays and worries, the endurance of which ought to qualify anyone for a diploma in the virtue of patience at the most exacting university, we at length emerged from the place in a long single file. I led the way with Momo, a Hausa soldier whom I had brought with me from Lokoja as a servant, Dr. T., Salam, and the horse bringing up the rear, and Bonner looking after the centre. Soon after leaving the village the path became from six to ten inches wide, and commenced to wind in a northerly direction through thinly wooded country with grass from four to six feet high. We had in all fifty-one carriers, the first twenty-five of whom wished to walk from three and a half to four miles an hour, whilst the last six or eight objected to go more than one or two miles in the same time, the rest of the fifty-one being desirous of proceeding at various intermediate paces. The difficulty of keeping the men together was almost insuperable, and became more so the further we got away from Loko. After rather more than an hour's march along a narrow but perfectly dry path we had to wade up to our waists in water in crossing a creek. My watertight boots proved to be very much more watertight than one could have wished them to be, as the water which got in from the tops remained swishing about in them to the end of our march. We halted three times in order to give our carriers a rest and at the same time to enable the hindermost men, who were often as much as ten or fifteen minutes behindhand, to come up. This tendency to scatter is the more distressing in view of the reports which we have received as to the possibility of our being waylaid and suddenly attacked by natives armed with poisoned arrows. About 1 P.M., when the heat of the sun had already become very trying, we reached a small village of some two hundred inhabitants, called Wisherogo, on an open space in which we put up our tents. Soon after our arrival our carriers, or rather their two headmen, came to say that the loads, which as a matter of fact were considerably below the average weight, were too heavy for them, and that they could not, or rather would not, proceed any further with us. As we were completely in the power of the carriers—all of them having received a bag of salt in advance, which would be a dead loss to us in the event of their deserting—I had to give in to their demands, and after some considerable discussion agreed to hire two more carriers from here to Nassarawa so as to lighten the loads a little all round. During our march to-day I carried a Winchester repeating rifle and a Colt's frontier revolver, which takes the same cartridge; Dr. T. carried the same; Bonner carried a Martini-Henry rifle and a revolver; Salam a double-barrelled gun, which, however, we thought it safer to leave unloaded. We had with us also two more Martini and two double express sporting rifles. According to our aneroid we have risen 290 feet, and are now 715 feet above sea-level. Dr. T., who took charge of the rear to-day, had by far the most trying post. It is quite a common occurrence for a man to hitch his load up in a tree or to place it on the ground and declare his inability to go a step further. At one place towards the end of to-day's march one man put down his load ten times within about a hundred yards, on each occasion requiring assistance in order to get his load on to his head again.

September 15.—Got up at 4.15 in the hope of making an early start. Having spent a long time in packing up our goods so as to be ready for the march, we were informed that two of our porters had deserted us, and had been seen going back to Loko. (Later on we discovered that this was a lie invented for the purpose of preventing us from starting.) It further transpired that the two additional carriers, for whom I had arranged yesterday, were not forth-coming. Yet again we were informed that our horse had become so ill during the night that it was impossible for it to proceed without at least a day's rest. This latter piece of information proved to be all too true, as on examining the horse it became evident that many days would have to elapse before it would be capable of continuing its travels. The trouble is that we cannot sell it, as its value in cowries would require fifteen extra porters to carry, to whom we should have to pay all the money they carried and a great deal more besides; there is in fact nothing which we could get in exchange for it which it would pay to carry with us.

September 16.—Started at 7 A.M. after having been compelled to engage four extra carriers, thus making up our number to fifty-six. Abandoned our horse as it was quite unfit to travel. About a quarter of a mile after starting we had to wade through water for some considerable distance, from two to three feet deep; we then came to the river Keraka, through which it would have been impossible to wade, and across which a rough but picturesque bridge made of twigs and branches had been constructed. After crossing this we had another long piece of wading to do. Two or three large dog-faced monkeys were sitting watching us on the trees. Soon after this it became evident that one of our porters was utterly

NATIVE BRIDGE ACROSS RIVER KERAKA.

The two trees which form part of the bridge are *in situ*; the central portion is composed of a dead trunk. The water below is very deep.

[*To face page* 46.]

incapable of carrying any load however light. Having discharged this man as incapable I found it impossible to make any provision for the carriage of his load. The difficulty was however at length surmounted by my distributing as a free gift to the carriers the contents of a bag of rice weighing fifty-five pounds. After marching for two or three hours I halted in order to allow the men in the rear to come up; it was nearly an hour before they did so. Whilst waiting for them I discovered that the place at which I was proposing to halt to-night had no water; our idiotic guide had failed to tell us this before, although he knew perfectly well that we were intending to go there. Our carriers on receiving this information became very excited and angry. It certainly would have been a most awkward position to have found oneself in, had we succeeded in reaching the place for which we were marching with fifty-five angry carriers and not a drop of water for them to drink. I decided accordingly to pitch our camp at the point we had already reached, a small supply of dirty water being available not far off. Having chosen a spot for camping, the men proceeded to construct for themselves a set of bomas or huts made from the branches of trees; these they erected in a circle round our tent. The only food which we have with us now is native rice and guinea corn; the latter is certainly most unappetising.

The greater part of our way to-day lay through thinly wooded country, though at times the path led for a while through dark primeval forest. We passed a large number of ant-hills, six to eighteen feet high; from some of those which were in ruin we could see that they had a corresponding underground excavation, four to six feet deep. As we are liable to be attacked either by men or beasts we have to take it in turns to keep watch during the night. Before we turned in our carriers came to say that the week's subsistence money, which was served out to them three days ago, was exhausted, and that they had nothing now to eat. For unconscionable greed and ingratitude it would be difficult to surpass this last demand. We agreed at Lokoja to pay our carriers as subsistence money two thousand cowries per week; as we were in the act of starting we gave them provision for three days; when two only out of these three days had elapsed we paid them a week's subsistence money in advance, since which we have provided them twice with meat at our expense; and lastly, but a few hours have elapsed since we divided fifty-five pounds of rice amongst them as an additional gift. It is scarcely necessary to record the reception which this demand met with.

From the above extracts the reader will gather a very fair idea of the ordinary routine difficulties which have to be overcome in a march such as that on which we were engaged. As in other parts of the continent, so here, the one unceasing trouble is the management of the native carriers. It is indeed almost impossible for any one who has not had personal dealings with African porters to realise the worries and vexations which their employment involves. Had we been travelling as Arabs, or as rich natives of the country would travel, these difficulties would not have occurred, or would at any rate have been reduced to a minimum. The carriers which such a traveller would take with him would be almost exclusively slaves, some his personal property, others perhaps the property of a friend or travelling companion. In the event of any carrier refusing to march he would be liable to be punished or even killed on the spot, or could be sold in the market at any place *en route*. The very fact that the natives know that the white man will under no circumstances buy or sell a man as a slave makes them eager to join his caravan, but at the same time renders it impossible for the European to gain any really effective control over them. Mr. Joseph Thomson who, before travelling in West Africa, had had considerable experience of Swahili porters on the East Coast, writes during the course of his journey to Sokoto :—

"For three weeks Seago and I have had a soul-sickening fight for the mastery with our entire

E

caravan, and in the course of it we have had to brandish our revolvers like transpontine stage brigands, use our fists and our tongues like natives of Billingsgate and hourly tear the passions to tatters, while our men have jeered at, threatened to murder us, and in a thousand ways to frighten us and bring our plans to contemptible failure. . . . Inwardly I devoutly wished that I had a caravan of Swahili porters, whom, in my want of knowledge, I had in other days wantonly reviled." * Considered as carriers the Hausas are immeasurably superior to the Nupes and Yorubas. Whilst the latter will grumble at having to carry fifty to sixty pounds, the former will often carry twice that weight with less than half the amount of grumbling. When we were in the act of setting out from Zaria to Kano, knowing that we should have none but Hausas as carriers, we made up our loads in ninety pound packs; when the carriers came in to feel the weight of their loads prior to bargaining for wages, half-a-dozen of them, on feeling the weight of a ninety-pound pack, put it down disdainfully and asked to be allowed to carry two, on the understanding, of course, that they would thus earn double wage. The only real difficulty which these seemed to experience was in setting down and picking up their loads. They usually waited till two of the single load carriers came to their aid before

* Cf. 'Good Words,' 1886, p. 250.

attempting to lift or put down their own loads. The reader will the more easily realise the weight of a hundred-and-eighty-pound pack when he is reminded that this is exactly three times the weight of luggage allowed to a third-class passenger on an English railway.

As may be gathered further from the above extracts, another difficulty, or at least serious inconvenience, which we met with on our march up from Loko, was due to the large number of streams and swamps through which we had to wade. The rainy season in this district begins towards the end of May and lasts till the middle or end of October. It would therefore have been better for us, as far as travelling was concerned, had we reached the Binué two months later than we did. On the other hand the most unhealthy part of the year is the time when the rains have just ended and the swamps and marshes are rapidly drying up. As it was, no member of our party became at all seriously ill during the course of our six weeks' march to Zaria, despite the fact that scarcely a day passed without our having several times to wade through water or soft mud nearly up to our waists, the result being that our feet were scarcely ever dry, as no sooner had they begun to be so than another stream or marsh appeared to wet them again.

A difficulty which would perhaps suggest itself to

anyone unacquainted with tropical Africa, but which is in reality of very infrequent occurrence, is that of losing one's way in the forest and so failing to arrive at one's destination for the night. The following quotation from Professor Drummond's 'Tropical Africa,' though written as a description of East Africa, is so exactly applicable to the country through which we passed that I need make no apology for inserting it :—

"It may be a surprise to the unenlightened to learn that probably no explorer in forcing his passage through Africa has ever, for more than a few days at a time, been off some beaten track. Probably no country in the world, civilised or uncivilised, is better supplied with paths than this unmapped continent. Every village is connected with some other village, every tribe with the next tribe, every state with its neighbour, and therefore with all the rest. The explorer's business is simply to select from this network of tracks, keep a general direction, and hold on his way. Let him begin at Zanzibar, plant his foot on a native footpath and set his face towards Tanganyika ; in eight months he will be there ; he has simply to persevere. From village to village he will be handed on, zigzagging it may be somtimes to avoid the impassable barriers of nature or the rarer perils of hostile tribes, but never taking to the woods, never guided solely by the stars, never in fact leaving

a beaten track, till hundreds and hundreds of miles
are between him and the sea, and his interminable
footpath ends with a canoe on the shores of
Tanganyika. . . . The native tracks which I have just
described are the same in character all over Africa.
They are veritable footpaths, never over a foot in
breadth, beaten as hard as adamant, and rutted
beneath the level of the forest bed by centuries of
native traffic. . . . Although the African footpath is
on the whole a bee-line, no fifty yards of it are ever
straight. And the reason is not far to seek. If a
stone is encountered no native will ever think of
removing it. Why should he? It is easier to walk
round it; the next man who comes that way will
do the same. He knows that a hundred men are
following him, he looks at the stone a moment, and
it might be unearthed and tossed aside, but no; he
also holds on his way. It is not that he resents the
trouble, it is that the idea is wanting. . . . But it
would be a very stony country indeed, and Africa is
far from stony, that would wholly account for the
aggravating obliqueness and indecision of the African
footpath. Probably each four miles on an average
path is spun out by an infinite series of minor
sinuosities to five or six. Now these deflections are
not meaningless. Each has some history, a history
dating back perhaps a thousand years, but to which
all clue has centuries ago been lost. The leading

cause probably is fallen trees; when a tree falls across a path no man ever removes it. As in the case of the stone, the native goes round it. It is too green to burn in his hut; before it is dry and the white ants have eaten it, the new détour has become part and parcel of the path. . . . Whatever the cause, it is certain that for persistent straightforwardness in the general, and utter vacillation and irresolution in the particular, the African roads are unique in engineering."

To resume the actual story of our march : Five days from the time of our leaving Loko we arrived at the bank of a large fast-flowing river, which separated us from Nassarawa, and which at this point is called after the name of the town. The operation of ferrying our goods across in a native canoe occupied three hours. On landing on the far side of the river one of the first questions I was asked was whether we were bringing any gin with us; we were given to understand that in such case we should be the very opposite of welcome. We were fortunately able to give them the most positive assurances on this point, and expressed our fullest sympathy with their desire to exclude from their country what they called " the bad drink." The last of our loads having been ferried across, the representative of the king, who was himself absent on a slave raid, assigned us a residence in the town, to which we proceeded. Soon after our arrival the maigida, or master of the house, brought us a present of a turkey, some guinea corn, and some yams. As the only food we had eaten during the day was some cold rice, it having been impossible to make a fire in the morning in consequence of the rain, we killed and cooked the turkey with the very shortest possible delay. The following extracts from the diary will give some idea of the town and of our reception by its inhabitants :—

September 19.—We were awoke this morning by a poet singing in a stentorian voice a Hausa song of welcome. After singing for an inordinate length of time he came round to receive the present which he considered himself to have earned; we gave him a coloured handkerchief, but soon regretted having done so, as his success in extracting a present from us induced several more singers to attempt the same. We took however no steps to encourage them. The curiosity of the inhabitants at seeing three white men is excessive; a crowd of visitors thronged our house, or rather the court of it, nearly all day. Towards evening the royal executioner came to salute us, and obligingly drove them all away ! I showed our native guide a map of Hausaland. On my proceeding to name off in succession the places which lay along certain well-known routes, his astonishment knew no bounds, and he ran off to tell some of the others of the marvellous powers of the Englishman's paper. Many of the natives here have as a tribal mark one scar below each eye. The king's interpreter called and interpreted the Arabic letter which we had brought with us to the king from the Royal Niger Company. I showed him a copy of St. Matthew's gospel in Hausa, in which he seemed greatly interested.

September 20.—The height of Nassarawa above the sea according to our boiling-point thermometer is 557 feet, according to the aneroid 555 feet. A man professing to be a son of the Sultan of Sokoto arrived with a train of followers to pay us a call. He sat on and on, evidently determined not to go away until he had extracted a present from us. I greatly doubted his being a son of the Sultan at all, but as he fairly wore out our patience by the length of his visit, I gave him at last a small present in the hope of inducing him to go away. He however rejected my present with scorn, and after sitting for some considerable time further in the hope of our making a better offer, he went away in a most unsuitable frame of mind. There is a very pretty bird common here, the native name of which is jamberdé, about the size of a small sparrow; its neck and breast are bright scarlet, its tail dull red with brown tip, wings also brown. The king of Nassarawa is expected home from his war to-morrow, and it is evident that we shall have difficulty in getting away prior to his

return. Took a walk through the town this afternoon; the houses all stand in compounds, the walls of
which are for the most part made of thatch or grass
matting, the walls of the houses and those of the
king's compound being made of hardened mud. I
should think the population of the town would
probably be about ten thousand.

September 22.—Beggars innumerable keep coming to
ask for every imaginable thing. A
messenger from the king arrived
yesterday to say that he would
return to-day, and that we must
await his coming. Bought sixteen lemons for twenty cowries,
i.e., at the rate of 160 for a penny.
Another musician came to-night
who sang and beat his drum con-

HAUSA DRUM.

tinuously for an hour and three-quarters. As we
still showed no signs of giving him a present, a
request for which formed part of his song, he gave
us up as hopeless and retired. Hope to start
to-morrow morning unless forcibly prevented.

September 23.—After preparing all our loads in the
hope of getting away to-day, a deputation arrived to
say that the king was coming to-day and that we
could not go. I explained that, as we had already
become ill in consequence of staying here so long, we
could not and would not wait any more. On going,

however, to interview our carriers, they definitely
refused to start, and on my pressing them to do so,
forty-five of them, all of whom were Yorubas, started
up and said that they would leave and return to
Lokoja.　They proceeded to put their threat into
immediate execution by taking their things and
marching off on the way back to Loko.　I was forced,
though with considerable reluctance, to send a con-
ciliatory message after them in order to induce them
to return.　The two head men then explained that
had they consented to go with us, they would on
their return journey have had their heads cut off on
reaching this place.　The most distressing feature of
the case is that we do not in the least know when
the king will really return; it is quite possible that
he may not come for a week or even a month.

September 24.—We have now been detained here a
whole week awaiting the return of the king, during
which time we have had fifty-five hungry men to feed.
We were informed this morning that we ought to
send our present to the king beforehand to await his
arrival.　Accordingly I put out a silk Tunisian girdle,
a silk rug, a mirror and a Norwegian knife; this we
sent, but it was soon afterwards returned and we
were told that it was customary (as I knew before)
to give it to the king ourselves.　His people had
simply been impelled by curiosity to tell us lies in
regard to their customs in order that they might see

what sort of a present we intended giving. I sold
to-day an English shilling for two thousand cowries;
they are worn here set in rings on the finger, and are
in great demand for this purpose. The king arrived
about 2 P.M.; it appears that his attempted raid has
been a failure and that no slaves have been captured.
About 4.30 he sent to say that we might come to
see him. On spreading out the present which we
had brought with us, he pushed it from him and
declared that it was not sufficient. I said we were
poor and could not increase it; he replied that we
must. I said that in that case we would return to
Loko and tell the people of our country that he had
expelled us from his land; he at length grudgingly
accepted what we had offered. Sympathy is certainly
a virtue singularly undeveloped amongst the people
here. When, for example, we stated at our audience
with the king that the air of the place did not agree
with us, and that we had become ill in consequence of
our delay, his attendants simply burst out laughing
in our faces.

Having obtained permission from the king to leave,
we had intended starting the following morning but
were again prevented from doing so, this time by the
illness of one of my companions. On the next day
however, *i.e.*, September 25, we had the satisfaction of
leaving Nassarawa behind us, and after a march of

about fourteen miles halted for the night at a large village called Laminga. The mud house which was assigned to us here was unfortunately far from water-tight, and a violent rain and thunderstorm having come on, we spent a good part of the night under the shelter of our umbrellas. A farther march of about twelve miles brought us to Kaffi, a large town with a red mud wall ten or twelve feet high and several miles in circumference. Our supply of rice and other food having run out on the previous day, we had left Laminga without having been able to get any satis-factory breakfast, and on our arrival at Kaffi were, as can easily be imagined, something more than normally hungry. It was therefore a trial of patience worthy of Central Africa, to be compelled from one cause or another to wait for over seven hours after our arrival before obtaining anything definite to eat. Ten eggs, which we had bought *en route* in the hope of having something to cook immediately on our arrival, turned out without exception to be bad! Eggs in West Africa are scarcely ever eaten by the natives; when, then, a traveller expresses a desire for them, the natives proceed to disturb the various sitting hens that they can find in the neighbourhood, in order to sell their half-hatched progeny to the white men. As time went on we became more skilful in testing eggs beforehand, the most certain test, as we found, being to hold them up to the sun;

should they then appear light coloured and nearly transparent, they are almost certainly good, but not otherwise. Another test, though by no means equally satisfactory, is to place them in water; if they sink they are probably good, and if they float, bad.

The altitude of Kaffi, according to our aneroid and boiling-point thermometer, is just a thousand feet above sea-level. The market is considerably larger than that of Nassarawa, the principal objects on sale being yams, rice, plantains, native tobacco, guinea corn, salt both native and English, pepper, kola nuts, a sort of loose earth used as soap, two different kinds of roots from which oil is obtained, cotton from the silk-cotton tree, native and English cloth, and sugar-canes; these last are only used for chewing, the natives being apparently entirely ignorant of the possibility of obtaining sugar therefrom. During our stay here we witnessed for the first time a sight with which we were afterwards to become all too familiar, viz., a large number of slaves exposed for sale in the open market. We were detained in Kaffi no less than ten days, owing to the difficulty which we experienced in obtaining sufficient cowries to give to our carriers as food-money. There being no shops or wholesale dealers, we had to employ men to carry our cloth round in the market, selling it by retail until the required number of cowries,

viz., two hundred and twenty thousand, were obtained. This number would represent about £6 in
English money, and would weigh about a thousand
pounds.　　Besides cloth, we sold here a certain
number of Maria Theresa dollars, for which we obtained about three shillings and sixpence worth of
cowries. This coin, which is made in Vienna and
bears date 1780, is manufactured exclusively for export
to Central Africa. It passes to a certain extent in
Tripoli, though the Turks make every effort to
exclude it, but in the Western Soudan, and more
especially in the Hausa States, it is almost everywhere current, and has been so for at least half a
century. Had we realised beforehand the extent to
which it would pass, we should have relied far more
on it and far less upon cloth than we did. It contains about two shillings' worth of silver, and its
purchasing value in the Soudan varies from three to
four shillings and sixpence.

Civilisation, or, I should perhaps say, the evils of
civilisation, have become so far developed in Kano
that counterfeit dollars, chiefly composed of lead, are
from time to time manufactured there, one of which
I succeeded in obtaining as a curiosity. It is greatly
to be hoped that the importation of this dollar may
ere long be largely increased, as one of the chief
hindrances to the development of trade in the interior
is the lack of any really portable currency.

CHAPTER V.

KAFFI TO ZARIA.

THE distance from Loko to Kaffi is somewhat under
eighty miles, while that from Kaffi to Zaria, our
next important stopping-place, is about one hundred
and eighty more. After leaving Kaffi our route
lay for some time through very hilly country, the
inhabitants of which are for the most part pagans,
many of them moreover being said to be cannibals.
Though situated within the territory of Zaria, many
of these villages pay little or no tribute, their position, often on the summits of inaccessible hills,
rendering it impossible for the king of Zaria to exact
it from them by force. As far as it was possible to
ascertain, all these people speak the Hausa language,
though their origin would appear to be distinct from
that of the Hausas generally. One day's march from
Kaffi brought us to a village which bore the
euphonious name of Jimbambororo. Here the trouble
with the carriers who had come with us from Lokoja,
and whose demands had been gradually becoming
more and more exorbitant, came at last to a definite

crisis. The account is perhaps best given in the words of the diary :—

October 8.—Got up at 4 A.M. in the hope of making an early start. As we were engaged in packing up, one of our carriers announced his intention of leaving us. As he was evidently unwell and incapable of carrying his load, there was nothing for it but to agree to his proposal. I accordingly wrote him out an order payable at Lokoja for one bag of salt, which was rather more than what was actually due to him. Some of his friends amongst the other carriers insisted that I should give him three times this amount, and on my refusing to do so, all the Yorubas, including our two head men, struck and, untying their loads which they had already prepared for carrying, threatened to desert us unless their demand was immediately complied with. A most violent scene now ensued. I told the Yorubas that they were free to go back to Lokoja, but that in the event of their doing so they would none of them receive any orders for salt. I owe them now one bag each. After vainly endeavouring to overawe us into complying with their demand, thirty-one of them left, having assured us that we should all be killed before a day had passed. Thirteen of the men from Lokoja, all of whom are Nupés, have remained with us, and declared their willingness to go on. With the Hausas I have thus twenty-three, but, require fifty-four. I have accordingly sent one of the most trust-worthy of our men back to Kaffi with instructions to hire, if possible, sufficient men to replace those who have deserted us.

2.30 P.M.—Twelve of our runaway carriers have just reappeared and expressed their willingness to accompany us; they say that the other twenty, including the sick man, have gone back to Kaffi.

October 9.—Our messenger whom we had sent to Kaffi reappeared this morning, followed by a large number of would-be carriers. He said that our twenty men had already left Kaffi on their return journey to Lokoja : a statement which was however almost immediately refuted by the appearance of the carriers themselves. They brought with them the man in whose house we had stayed at Kaffi, and a message from the maigajia, *i.e.*, the prime minister of the king, to whom they had apparently appealed for help against us, begging us to take them back. This, however, I absolutely refused to do, or even to discuss the question further. On going out to interview the newly-arrived men from Kaffi, I found that they had no food or cowries with them, neither of which I could provide for another week, *i.e.*, until our arrival at Katchia. They, however, agreed to accept as food-money a roll of cloth, for which the people of the village would pay them six thousand cowries. This gives each man three hundred

F

cowries, *i.e.*, about three halfpence, as provision-money
for the following week. In addition to this I agreed
to pay each man twenty thousand cowries, or about ten
shillings, for the carriage of his load to Zaria, distant
one hundred and eighty miles; this amount to be
payable on arrival there.

October 10. — On leaving Jimbambororo, the
country through which we passed had at first
occasional patches of cultivation; after a short time
it resumed its normal aspect, *i.e.*, thinly wooded land
with high grass at intervals, and later on we passed
for a short time through dense forest. After going
about five miles we came to a spot where, two days
ago, fifteen native merchants were attacked and
carried off as slaves. Shortly before this we passed
thirty men fully armed in native style, with bows and
poisoned arrows, carrying no loads, but apparently
on the look-out for some one to relieve of theirs.
As we were at the moment marching in close order,
one behind the other, with our limited stock of
rifles displayed to the best advantage, they made no
attempt to molest us. After going about eleven
and a half miles we arrived at Gitata, to reach
which we had to ascend a very steep rocky incline,
the hill on which the village is built rising in all
some 1500 feet above the plain. On our arrival we
had our luggage placed down close to a huge silk-
cotton tree, under the shade of which a large and

CROSSING A RIVER.

[To face page 67.

noisy market was being held. Amongst the people in the market we noticed about twenty cases of *goître*, some extravagantly developed. Before it became dark a most weird scene was enacted close to us, and apparently for our benefit. A wild shrieking crowd advanced, carrying a pole fifteen feet long, with a sort of cow-bell fastened on the top, and brandishing two or more live vultures, which they proceeded to hack to pieces in a most savage manner. This was, I presume, some native pagan ceremony, though we were unable to ascertain its origin or meaning.

October 11.—Had to wade to-day through an unusual amount of water, including five streams of considerable size. The largest—about twelve miles after leaving Gitata—is, I believe, the same river that we crossed at Nassarawa; at the point at which we crossed it, it had a width of about 110 yards, and a very rapid current. On reaching the village of Panda, where we had decided to halt for the night, we were assigned a house, or rather a room, in which were hung up a number of gigantic leather shields, about five feet high and four feet across; they seemed almost too heavy for a single man to carry.

On leaving Panda, a march of four days through much the same sort of country as has been above described, brought us to Katchia, the only place of any importance between Kaffi and Zaria. From Kaffi to Katchia the country tends steadily to rise, the latter place being no less than 2440 feet above sea-level. Our route for several days lay through extremely rough and hilly country, the most common rock being grey granite and gneiss ; we passed also several very curious-looking sugar-loaf hills from 800 to 1200 feet in height, one or two of which were almost entirely bare and far too precipitous to climb. One river of considerable size, across which we had to be ferried in canoes, lies about seventeen miles to the south of Katchia ; its native name is Gurara, its course at the point at which we crossed being from east to west.

The inhabitants of this district, many of whom wear no clothes of any kind, whilst others are content with a girdle of leaves, are a most degraded and unintelligent-looking set of people. According to the statements of our carriers, many of them are cannibals, though we were not able to obtain any definite proof of this fact. Although they seemed all to speak the Hausa language, we found it extremely difficult to hold any intercourse with them, as they were evidently suspicious of us, and no doubt thought that, if opportunity offered, we should attempt to carry some of them off as slaves. This part of the country is generally regarded as unsafe, except for numerous and well-armed caravans. In order to share the protection of our rifles, a hundred and fifty other natives attached themselves to us, most of whom were engaged in carrying English imported salt up the country. They marched as a rule immediately in front of us, but caused us constant trouble, as two or three of them at a time would stop and rest for a few minutes and then try to insert themselves in our caravan, thus lengthening our line of carriers, and so rendering us less secure in case of an attack. On approaching Katchia we saw, for the first time since entering the Niger, several small herds of cows. The keeping of cattle is almost exclusively confined throughout the Hausa States to the Fulahs, who, as we shall see later on, are easily distinguishable from the Hausas by their general features and expression. Although in some parts large herds of cows are kept, it is seldom possible, as we found to our distress, to obtain such a thing as fresh milk. The natives do not regard milk as fit to drink, and therefore as saleable, until it has become sour.

We had hoped to have been able to pass Katchia without any delay, but, partly owing to the importunity of the king for a larger present than I was willing to give, and partly owing to further trouble with our carriers, we were compelled to stay for four days. On the morning following our arrival, I went with Dr. T. to salute the king, and took with me the present which I had intended for him. He proved to be the most greedy personage with whom we had till then had to deal, and professed to regard my present as totally beneath his dignity to accept. Knowing that he was himself subject to the king of Zaria, I tried to work upon his fears by telling him that I was the bearer of a letter addressed to the latter. He, however, replied that as the king of Zaria was at present away from his own town we must leave with him the letter, together with the present that was destined for Zaria. On my vehemently objecting to this proposal, he said that we must remain in Katchia until a messenger had been with a message from him to the king and had returned again. On regaining our house I sent to him the letter which was addressed to Zaria, with a message to say that I should inform the king that it had been extracted from us by force. Later on in the day our Hausa soldier came to inform us that a son of the king of Zaria, who happened to be staying here, had been to the king of Katchia, and had informed him that he was on no account to interfere with our departure, and that the letter must not be taken from us. A few minutes later this son of the king of Zaria himself appeared, in order to obtain from us the reward which he considered himself to have earned by his good offices on our behalf. On the second day after our arrival in Katchia, we received detailed information, which was confirmed from two different sources, to the effect that from three to four thousand of the hill tribes between this and Zaria, having heard of the approach of some white men with a large quantity of goods, had arranged to waylay us at a certain point which it would be impossible to avoid passing. The situation was certainly not altogether encouraging, as in the event of a determined attack, we had every reason to suspect that our carriers would one and all consult their personal safety by running away as fast as their legs could carry them. Subsequent experience proved that this suspicion was not groundless. Moreover, from a brigand's point of view the country here was simply an ideal one, as the narrow path, winding at one time through grass eight to ten feet high, and at another time through dense forest, afforded unlimited opportunities for a sudden and successful attack. Happily for us, as it eventually proved, it was obviously our duty to adhere to our original plan. Nothing would have been gained by waiting, there was no one to appeal to for assistance, and to turn back would have been to sacrifice the whole results of our work. Having therefore drilled one or two picked men amongst our carriers in the use of a rifle, we continued our preparations for starting at the earliest moment it should prove possible to do so. On October 19, four days after our arrival in Katchia, we set out in earnest for Zaria, distant rather less than a hundred miles. The following are a few further extracts from the diary :—

October 19.—On leaving the town we were accompanied by a very large number of people, most of whom were carriers, who had apparently been waiting for our departure in order that they might use us as their escort. One of them carried a flint-lock gun, and another had an old Snider ; these were all the firearms which they appeared to possess. We marched fairly fast and waded through five streams ; after going about six miles the path began gradually to descend, still keeping an almost exactly northerly direction. After passing a magnificent sugar-loaf rock on our left, about 2.30 P.M. we reached the village of Katill, the people of which, crowding around us, showed every disposition to steal some of our possessions. To-morrow we are due to reach the spot where the brigands are supposed to be awaiting us.

October 20.—1 A.M. Keeping watch from twelve to two. Ruminating on the prospect of our getting to the end of our journey to-day. I suppose if we do not, this diary will get lost. Four men left here a few minutes ago armed and carrying no loads ; possibly they are going to report concerning us to their friends ahead. 6 P.M. We started at six this morning ; half an hour's delay was caused at the start by the dawdling of our crowd of uninvited companions, who blocked the path in front of us. After going about five miles we came to a miserable-looking village called Adimanzaure, immediately beyond which was a river which bears the same name. The march was very long and tiring; hour after hour we kept the most careful look-out in the long grass and amidst the woods for our friends the brigands, but I am most thankful to say they failed to make themselves visible. Momo, our Hausa servant, at one point picked up a poisoned arrow lying just in front of me, but this had not been aimed at us but at some previous traveller. After going nearly seventeen miles we halted for the night on a large exposed rock just beyond another small village.

October 22.—The people through whose country we are now passing belong to the Kedara tribe; prior to this our route for about fifty miles lay through the country of the Kedje, who are for the most part professional brigands; few of them wear anything more than a girdle of leaves or a piece of skin. During to-day's march we crossed the river Koduna; at the point at which we reached it, it was about four hundred yards wide and flowing N.N.W.; according to the French map of this district, it turns later on S.S.W., and, passing a little north of Bida, joins the Niger about a hundred and twenty miles above Lokoja. Two canoes were available to help us across. The boatman took us about a hundred

yards and then left us to wade the rest. Stayed for
the night in a large village called Gierko, just beyond
the river. We have now passed the country which
is considered unsafe, and are within about forty miles
of Zaria.

October 24.—Crossed to-day another river about
eighty yards wide called Shika; as only two very
small canoes were available the crossing occupied
three hours and a half. Whilst sitting on the far
side waiting for the rest to arrive, I was showing to
one of our carriers the working of a Winchester rifle.
About half-a-dozen more of the carriers were sitting
in a semicircle opposite, distant perhaps a couple of
yards. One of these was leaning his arm against
a tin trunk which contained our canteen. The
mechanism of the rifle, which was an old one, must
have been defective, for it suddenly went off; the
bullet passed between his arm and heart and pierced
right through the trunk, seriously injuring a large
number of our cooking and other utensils. The man
rolled backwards incontinently into the bush, doubtless imagining that he was "kilt entirely," his companions being at the same time seized with almost
equal panic. This incident afforded our carriers an
exciting subject of conversation for several days afterwards, and quite a number of natives to whom they
had retailed the story came wanting to be allowed to
examine the hero of the event, *i.e.*, the canteen.

Three miles beyond this river we reached a small town called Igabe, where we are halting for the night. Hope to reach Zaria to-morrow.

October 25.—Further trouble with the carriers, twenty of whom refused to start. As the rest expressed their willingness to accompany me, I arranged to go on with these, leaving Dr. T. and Bonner, the latter of whom was unwell, to follow. As soon, however, as we were ready to set out, a scene of the utmost noise and violence commenced, which lasted for very nearly an hour. By the end of this time the rest of the carriers, by threatening to murder those who were prepared to start, so over-awed them that they too refused to move. We are thus compelled to sit down and spend the day here.

October 26.—After a march of seventeen miles we arrived about 2 P.M. at the gates of Zaria. As we had been obliged to wade through some five or six streams and were not a little wet by the time we reached the gate, it was no small trial of our patience to be kept waiting there for two hours and a quarter before being allowed to proceed to the house assigned to us. Immediately upon our arrival a native, who turned out to be a Kroo boy, came up to me and seemed exceedingly anxious to impart some information. As I failed to understand the language he was using, I inquired if he could speak either Hausa or Arabic. Finding that he understood neither, I

passed him on to Dr. T., who eventually elicited the
fact that the language in which he had been speaking
was English !

The substance of the information which the Kroo
boy had to impart was that there was another white
man in the town who was very ill and desired to
see us immediately. Dr. T., though tired with the
long march, went at once to see who this might be,
and what assistance we could afford him. The white
man proved to be a young Canadian who had left
Lagos ten months before, and, travelling as a sort of
independent missionary, had succeeded in making
his way up as far as this *viâ* Bida and Birnin Gwari.
He had been provided in the first instance with a
totally inadequate supply of goods, including no
firearms, and on reaching Birnin Gwari the king
had stolen from him nearly everything which he
possessed. He was suffering from chronic dysentery
at the time of our arrival at Zaria, and it was
obvious that his only chance of life was to start at
once for the coast. His immediate wants were
supplied and sufficient resources given him by us to
enable him to reach the river Niger. He started
a few days later in company with some of our
carriers who were returning to Lokoja, but after
going three days' march he died, to our great regret,
at Gierko, about forty miles south of Zaria.

Whilst one cannot but admire intensely the zeal and self-sacrifice which could induce a man, knowing nothing of any native language, without an interpreter and with no previous experience of travelling in Africa, to undertake to preach Christianity to the Mohammedans of the Central Soudan, one cannot but regret that all ordinary precautions, necessary, humanly speaking, to give such an enterprise a chance of success, were thought either unnecessary or undesirable. There is, perhaps, no part of Africa where a traveller, without very considerable resources, would find it more difficult to make his way, or where he would find it more impossible to earn a living, as this good man had expected to be able to do, by carpentry or any other craft. The traveller is expected to give a present to the king or chief of every village at which he stays, and, should he be unable to do so, will meet with a most ungracious reception. In the first large town at which he attempts to stay, he will probably have the very necessaries of life stolen from him in default of the expected present, and, should he succeed in reaching a second, he would probably be expelled with insult.

The house which was assigned to us in Zaria, consisting as it did of three well-built huts and an outside porch, was the best we had as yet stayed in. This was the more satisfactory as we proposed to halt here for some considerable time.

CHAPTER VI.

ZARIA.

ZARIA was the first really important town in the Soudan visited by us during the course of our expedition. It might be worth while, therefore, to pause for a short time in order very briefly to describe the past history, in so far as it has been ascertained, and the present political condition of that part of the Soudan in which Zaria and the other Hausa States are situated.

First, then, in regard to the use of the actual word Soudan. The word, which means simply the black country, *i.e.*, the country of the blacks, is applied by the natives themselves to the whole of the vast region south of the Great Sahara and north of the equator, stretching from the river Nile on the east to the Atlantic Ocean on the west. To the Hausa States, which occupy about the middle of this immense area, may perhaps be most correctly assigned the expression "Central Soudan." The word Soudan would appear to bear in some parts a far more limited significance, as one of the kings through whose territory we passed after leaving Kano, bears the title, king of the Soudan. This title, however, though in general use even outside his own territory, probably originated as an expression of absurd flattery.

One characteristic common to the whole of the Soudan is the possession of two distinct seasons, a dry season of seven months', and a rainy season of five months' duration, the latter corresponding, roughly speaking, to the European summer. The rivers which flow through it, the Bahr el Ghazel, the Shari, the Niger and the Senegal, rise at comparatively low elevations, and are fed almost exclusively by surface-drainage from the rains.

Hausaland, or the country inhabited by the Hausa people, is composed of the following states, all of which are subject and tributary to one or other of the two which come first in the list : Sokoto, Gando, Gober, Kano, Kwontagora, Zaria, Katsena, Yakubu (more often called by the natives Garim Bautshi), and Adamawa. In addition to these, the two states of Bida and Borgu, though their inhabitants for the most part do not speak the Hausa language, are tributary either to Sokoto or Gando. The rulers of all these states are of a totally different race to the people over whom they rule. They are variously called Fulah, Fulbe, Fullatah and Fulani, and are, as a rule, easily recognisable from the Hausas by certain

definite physical characteristics. The colour of the
skin is a shade lighter; they are, as a rule, taller; the
nose is more aquiline in shape, and the hair somewhat less woolly than is the case with the Hausas.
Their mental and moral characteristics, moreover, are
almost equally distinct. Whilst the Fulahs are a
shrewd and intriguing race of soldiers and diplo-
matists, caring little for trade but passionately
desirous of obtaining for themselves dominion and
power, the Hausas are a quiet commercial people,
who carry their manufactures far beyond the limits
of their own country, but with little or no ambition
to interfere with the political constitution of the
countries in which they trade. The Fulahs were in
former time a race of shepherds, or rather herdsmen,
and even at the present day nearly all the cattle of
the country are in their possession. They are again
essentially an equestrian race, and to their proficiency
on horseback, in a country for the most part sufficiently open to allow of the effective use of cavalry, is
probably to be in a large measure ascribed the success
of a people whose numbers were utterly insignificant
compared with the race whom they conquered. The
history of the Fulahs prior to their appearance in
Hausaland is extremely uncertain. About two centuries ago they began to establish themselves in
small scattered communities throughout the districts
which now form the Sokoto empire. Though pro-

fessing Mohammedanism, they seem to have made
but little effort to convert the Hausas, who were
pagans, till the year 1802, when the sheik Othman
proclaimed a sort of religious war, and after many
reverses succeeded in consolidating, and establishing
himself as ruler over, the greater part of the present
Sokoto empire. On the death of Othman, in 1817,
the empire was divided up between his son Mohammed Bello and his brother Abd Allah. The
former, who took the title Sarikin Mussulmi, *i.e.*,
commander of the faithful, obtained by far the larger
and more important section, including Kano, Katsena,
Zaria, etc., his capital being Sokoto ; whilst the latter
ruled from his capital Gando over the south-western
portion of the original empire. Strange to say, this
arrangement, which, considering the close proximity
of Sokoto and Gando, might naturally have been
expected to give rise to continual friction, has lasted
unimpaired to the present day, one reason for its
continuance no doubt being that the rulers of Gando
have always acknowledged the spiritual, if not tem-
poral, superiority of the Sultan of Sokoto. There
has been therefore, in one sense, but a single ruler
over the whole Fulah empire. The kings of the
various Hausa States at the present time are so far
subject to Sokoto or Gando, that they are compelled
to pay a very considerable annual tribute, and are at
the same time under an obligation to furnish, when

G

called upon to do so, an armed contingent in the event of war. Subject, however, to the above limitations, the kings of the various provinces are free to make their own laws, to keep their own armies, and to raise what taxes they please. The Sultan of Sokoto is supposed to possess a veto on the appointment by the various states of their kings, but this veto is but rarely exercised. The events, which had been taking place in Kano immediately prior to our arrival at Zaria, will illustrate the difficulty which the Sultan finds in enforcing his claim to interfere with the choice by any state of their king. At the end of 1892 Bello, who had been king for many years, died. He was succeeded by a man named Tukr, whose cruelty and misgovernment soon created the greatest possible dissatisfaction amongst his people, the final result being that a rival candidate to the throne, a man named Isufu, determined to attempt an insurrection. Isufu and his friends began by retiring outside the town of Kano and raiding some two hundred of the villages subject to Kano which had previously given in their allegiance to Tukr. Having sold the inhabitants of all these villages as slaves, Isufu became sufficiently powerful to venture an attack upon the capital. He met here with but a faint-hearted resistance and succeeded in establishing himself upon the throne, Tukr and his friends having retreated into the open country. He had, however, barely made himself king before he fell ill and died, and was succeeded by his brother Baba. On being expelled from Kano, Tukr appealed for help to his liege lord the Sultan of Sokoto. The Sultan ordered the people of Kano to reinstate him, and, finding that they had no intention of complying with his request, he sent a body of troops to assist Tukr in the recovery of his kingdom. The king in possession at Kano appealed for help to the surrounding states and received promises of support from several of his brother kings. It being at length obvious that the restoration of Tukr would involve far more fighting than the Sultan at all cared to undertake, he abandoned his cause, and confirmed the appointment of Baba after receiving from him pledges for the payment of the customary annual tribute. At the time of our arrival in Zaria fighting was still going on outside Kano, and it seemed for some time doubtful whether it would be possible for us to visit the city.

To turn from the history of Hausaland in general to that of Zaria in particular. The rulers of Zaria, although Fulahs, belong apparently to quite a different branch of the race to that of the other Fulah kings. They are members of two ruling families, who take it in turn to nominate a successor to the throne. The present king is a Beriberi or Bornuese Fulah; his successor will be a Wangarawa

Fulah. Whilst staying in Zaria, I obtained a Hausa translation of an old Arabic MS., which gave the history of the town for the last hundred and twenty years, from the time of the deposition of the Hausa kings, and the establishment of the Fulahs in their place. The Fulahs now in Zaria came from a district about halfway between Kano and Garim Bautshi, and, arriving at first in small numbers, gradually increased their influence until they were strong enough to make a successful attempt upon the kingdom. The establishment of Fulah rule at Zaria was thus some thirty years prior to its establishment throughout Hausaland generally. From the time of Musa, the first of the Fulah dynasty, twelve kings in all have reigned in Zaria. The state of Zaria includes all the country lying to the south of the town as far as the river Binué. The various towns and villages within this area pay tribute to the king of Zaria, who in turn pays tribute to the Sultan of Sokoto. According to the MS. just referred to, at the time of the Fulah usurpation of the kingdom a large number of the pagan Hausas retreated towards the mountainous districts to the south of the town, where they succeeded in maintaining their own independence. Probably, the whole or part of the hill tribes described in the last chapter are descended from these refugees.

On our arrival in Zaria, we found that the king

THREE FULAHS, ILLUSTRATING DIFFERENT WAYS OF WEARING TURBAN.

[To face page 81.

was absent on a slave raid, and was not expected back for some considerable time. We accordingly sent the present, which we had intended for the king, to the chief minister, the maigajia, who had been left in charge of the town, asking him to forward it to the king. This he duly promised to do; but, on second thoughts, having apparently come to the conclusion that our present would be more useful to himself than to the king, he failed to keep his promise. This, as will subsequently appear, caused us very considerable trouble and loss. Our first difficulty, after settling into our house, was to raise the sum which we needed in order to pay our carriers, and which amounted to nearly three-quarters of a million cowries. Our supply of English cloth was practically exhausted; we could find no ready sale for the silks that we had brought with us, and, though we had still a considerable quantity of barter goods of various descriptions, it was impossible to sell them quickly except at a ridiculous loss. The only thing that obtained a ready sale was camphor, a large quantity of which we sold. A block of camphor which can be bought in England for two-pence, sells here for rather more than a shilling. Besides camphor, we sold about one hundred and forty Maria Theresa dollars at five thousand cowries apiece, the result of which was that for some days afterwards the dollar was depreciated in value about

20 per cent., *i.e.*, from five thousand to four thousand
cowries. The value of the cowrie itself in Zaria is
considerably more than its value at Lokoja. As far
as it was possible to form an estimate in English
money, two thousand cowries, which at Lokoja were
equal in value to a shilling, were worth about one
shilling and fourpence at Zaria, and one shilling and
sixpence at Kano.

The time which we spent in Zaria was in all rather
less than two months. During nearly the whole of
this time I was engaged in the study of the Hausa
language, and more especially in the verification
and revision of the existing Hausa dictionary.
Dr. Tonkin very kindly undertook the task, which
was a far more laborious one than would naturally be
supposed, of selling our various barter goods in the
market, and of buying provisions and whatever else
we had need of from day to day. This set me free
to spend the best part of each day in study.

The town of Zaria, Zozo, or Zegzeg, as it is
variously called, contains a population of about
twenty-five or thirty thousand inhabitants.* It is
the capital of the largest province of the Sokoto
empire, including the towns of Kaffi, Nassarawa,
Loko, etc. It is surrounded by a mud wall of
perhaps ten miles in circumference, which, for

* Staudiger, who was in Zaria in 1886, estimates its population at from 50,000 to 100,000.

purposes of defence, would prove of but little use, as it is at present very much out of repair. Nearly half the space enclosed by the walls is cultivated land, on which is grown guinea corn, maize, and a few plantains; the rest of the space is occupied by houses built in courtyards, containing as a rule two or three huts apiece, the several huts serving in most instances as separate houses. They are built entirely of hardened mud, and thatched with coarse grass or reeds. In the market-place, which is very large, is to be found a wide selection both of native and imported goods and produce. A few specimens of the prices at which the goods in the market are sold, in so far as it is possible to make an estimate in English money, will serve to illustrate the present condition of trade, as well as the possibilities of its future development in this and the surrounding districts. Salt, which is one of the standards of exchange here, is sold at eighty thousand cowries, or £3, per half hundredweight, the price obtainable for English being just about the same as for native salt. Sugar cannot be obtained here unless specially ordered from Kano, where it fetches about one shilling and twopence the pound. Owing to the prohibition placed on the importation of firearms and ammunition by the Royal Niger Company, the price of cartridges, had we been willing to sell them, would have been ninepence per single cartridge of almost any pattern. Well-tanned leather made from goat skins sells at ninepence a piece. Swords made from native-wrought iron, for about three shillings each, whilst those brought from the east fetch more than double that price. Good riding horses can be obtained at prices ranging from fifteen shillings to six pounds apiece.

Lastly, slaves, of whom we saw as many as three hundred at one time on sale in the market-place, fetch from one hundred thousand to three hundred thousand cowries, or from three to nine pounds sterling. Slaves sold by private arrangement would probably fetch still higher prices.

The business and trade of the market were one day rudely interrupted during our stay in the town by a man named Bagudu, who, at the head of fifty horsemen, suddenly appeared in the place and commenced a raid upon the market, killing one man and wounding several more. Bagudu is one of the fairly innumerable sons of the Sultan of Sokoto, and supports himself by moving rapidly about the country, pillaging caravans and raiding small towns and villages. The absence of the king had probably emboldened him to make an attack upon so strong a town as Zaria. A little later than this, one of the messengers whom we despatched with letters for Lokoja fell into his hands, and was severely beaten by him. The letters were opened, but being written in English were considered valueless, the result being that our messenger eventually succeeded in recovering them, and delivering them safely at their destination.

The following extracts from the diary will give some further details of our life in Zaria :—

November 16.—Our supply of sugar having long since become exhausted, and there being little prospect of obtaining any more here, we decided yesterday to attempt the manufacture of sugar for ourselves. Accordingly, we bought fifty pieces of sugar-cane at fifty cowries apiece, and this morning we made our first attempt at manufacturing sugar. We began by fastening two tent-pegs together with a piece of wire, so as to make a sort of pair of nut-crackers. With this we crushed the sugar-cane, and found that a stick of cane about six feet long would produce a quart of liquid. This we boiled for some considerable time, till nothing was left but a hard substance closely resembling toffee, about one and a half pints of the liquid forming three ounces of the toffee. The mistake which we evidently made was in not straining away the treacle from the sugar during the operation of boiling. We had a visit to-day from an Arab who had travelled largely ; he had visited London, Paris, Jerusalem, etc. He seemed interested to find that I could give him so much information about the mosque of Omar in the latter place. Finished letter F in the dictionary to-day.

November 26.—Visited the indigo dye pits here. There are about fifty pits, thirty feet or more in depth, and carefully cemented round the sides. A sort of charcoal is mixed with the dye; the garments remain in the pits for periods varying from one to ten days. It is most curious to notice here that, although the market starts about sunrise, scarcely any business is done, and very few people attend till twelve or one o'clock, the very hottest part of the day. The same, I believe, holds true throughout the whole of Hausaland.

November 27.—Have adopted recently the native Hausa dress, as the wearing of it prevents one being constantly followed about by a crowd of inquisitive spectators, and renders it possible to mix freely with the common people. Dressed as Hausas, we are generally mistaken for Arabs, many of whose skins are quite as light as those of a European. Our room or hut is inhabited by countless numbers of mice, large and small lizards, beetles of varied size and colour, mosquitoes, ants, bats, and creeping things of names unknown; they walk, creep, crawl, hop, jump, and fly, both by night and by day. We have practically abandoned all attempts to control them. The lizards vary in length from about four to four-teen inches; they fortunately go to sleep at night, but during the daytime are exceedingly numerous and active.

November 28.—Dr. T. sold to-day, for twenty-five thousand cowries, about a dozen little bottles of scent. The materials employed in the composition of the scent were ammonia, turpentine, eucalyptus, and some medicated ointment which had gone bad, and had begun to emit a strong odour. These were sold to a dealer who will sell them again in the market. In this country, one has perpetually to suffer the mortification of discovering that really useful and expensive articles which one has brought with one, have to be sold for a much lower price than that paid for them, perhaps wholesale in London ; but this is to some extent counterbalanced by the fact that other things, which cost almost nothing at home, fetch marvellous prices here.

December 1.—Salam, our Arab boy, sleeps more soundly than anyone I have ever come across. It is a task of no ordinary magnitude to wake him once he is asleep. He tells a story in regard to himself to the effect that, one night, when travelling with an Arab in North Africa, he had to sleep with their donkey tethered to his leg to keep it from running away. When he woke in the morning it was to find that the donkey had wandered away to a considerable distance, dragging him along with it. Judging from our own experience of his sleeping powers, the story does not seem by any means incredible. I have been trying in vain to-day to get the Pole star into a new artificial horizon which I have just made; it seems impossible to take any star with my present apparatus lower than 23° above the horizon.

December 8.—The road to Kano being now open I have decided to go on there as soon as it is possible for us to start.

December 11.—Arranged to pay thirty-five carriers eight thousand cowries, or six shillings apiece for the carriage of our loads, weighing from eighty to ninety pounds each, to Kano, a distance of nearly a hundred miles. After having agreed to these terms, our prospective carriers went away, but ere long returned with the preposterous demand that the whole of their wages should be paid prior to starting. In the end I offered to pay them a proportion of their wages at the close of each day during the march. This they at first refused, but on the intervention of the owner of our house or rather his son, a man named Ali, they at length agreed to accept my offer. During the course of a speech which Ali made to them on this occasion, I heard him say, "We Hausas are all liars, but these English are not. If they say they like anyone they do so, if they say the opposite, they mean the opposite." It is thus arranged that we are to start early to-morrow morning.

December 12.—To-day has been a typical day of

attempted African travel. Our carriers had faithfully promised to start early this morning. We got up at 4.30 and made ready the loads. The carriers appeared about 6.15. Then began a series of disputing, lying, and thieving, which lasted nearly five hours, at the end of which time, having stolen five thousand six hundred of our cowries, they refused to start to-day at all. It would be difficult to imagine a more ideal scene for the exercise of patience. Really some one should paint a picture for the Academy to be called "Patience," with an African traveller sitting in a blazing sun with about fifty of the most ill-looking black specimens of humanity around him, each endeavouring to outdo his neighbour in the shamelessness of his demands. We had agreed to pay our carriers one thousand cowries each as food-money previous to starting; whilst engaged in doing so we handed them a sack containing fifteen thousand as food-money for fifteen men. During the operation of counting, they stole from this sack five thousand six hundred cowries, and then called our attention to the fact that the sack only contained nine thousand four hundred. We were compelled to make up the pretended deficiency. They now assure us that they will start without fail to-morrow morning.

December 13.—Yet another day of wearisome delay! As we were just about to start, a messenger arrived from the king to say that he was returning

to-day, and that we must await his arrival. We
tried in vain to induce our carriers to start, but as
they had been led to understand that the first man
who touched one of our loads would be forthwith
executed, it was not altogether surprising that our
solicitations were unheeded. The king entered the
town about 10 A.M., soon after which we received a
visit from an official of still higher rank than the
maigajia, who made a long speech with the object of
extracting a present from us. The title which this
man bore, sarikin makira, means literally king of the
blacksmiths. The blacksmiths in Zaria form a sort
of royal guild, and their head is a man of great
importance in the court. I replied that we had
already sent a large present to the king through the
maigajia, and that we could add nothing to it. A
little later on the sarikin makira sent us as a present
a miserable-looking kid, together with a little rice.
These I returned to him with a message to the effect
that I could receive no present until we had been
granted permission to leave the town.

December 14.—Dr. T. went to see the sarakin
makira this morning, and found him in a most im-
proper state of mind, in consequence of his present
having been returned last night. Dr. T., having become
somewhat excited, told him at length that he despised
both him and his present. He replied that he would
prevent our seeing the king, and therefore our leaving

the town for months to come. As matters were thus brought to a deadlock, it seemed best that Dr. T. should go back to the sarikin makira (as he himself suggested doing) and say that I disapproved of what had been said and that I desired to feel sweet towards him.

To make a long story short, by threatening to murder our carriers and so depriving us of our means of transport, and further by practically closing the market against us, the sarakin makira in the course of about three days succeeded in starving us into compliance with his demands. These consisted of the surrender to the king and to himself of goods to the value of about twenty five pounds, these being delivered up by us nominally as a present expressive of our goodwill. The custom of the country is that the present which a king gives to a visitor equals in value the present which he himself receives, but so completely was this custom ignored on this occasion, that for the exceptionally large present, which we were compelled to give, we received nothing whatever in return.

On December 16, we at length obtained the very real pleasure of turning our backs upon the people of Zaria, or rather upon their rulers, who are distinctly inferior to their subjects, and started in earnest for Kano.

The last night we spent in Zaria was rendered specially uncomfortable, owing to the invasion of our house, soon after midnight, by a countless host of small black ants with a particularly aggravating sting. These ants, called by the natives *kwari-kwassa*, travel long distances from place to place in search of food. They may often be seen crossing the path in the daytime in long compact lines, the larger soldier ants forming a kind of escort on either side of the procession. They move in a sort of bee-line across the country, no ditch or wall serving, even for a moment, to interrupt their march. Everything edible in the neighbourhood of their line of march is promptly devoured by them, after which they move on without leaving behind even a single straggler. As it was obviously impossible for us to wage war against them, we were compelled to beat an igno-minious retreat, and spent the rest of the night in a porch at a respectful distance from them. On returning to our house some four hours later, not a single trace of the invaders was to be seen.

CHAPTER VII.

ARRIVAL AT KANO.

UNTIL we were well outside the gate of Zaria it seemed quite uncertain as to whether we were to be allowed to leave, or whether some further excuse would not be invented for detaining us and relieving us of still more of our property. It was, then, with a feeling of no ordinary relief that we saw at last the town disappear behind us, and found ourselves once more in the open country. After a march of ten or eleven miles through fairly open country with patches of cultivation here and there, we arrived at a miserable-looking village called Likoro. The monotony of the one evening which we spent here was broken in the usual way, by a strike amongst our carriers, who came to demand that I should pay them one dollar, or five thousand cowries, each before proceeding any farther with our loads. On my refusing to do this they announced their intention of returning *en masse* to Zaria. We passed the night in complete uncertainty as to whether they would carry out their threat or not. On the following morning after a

H

discussion lasting several hours, finding that a certain number of the men were willing to proceed, I
made a start with all who were prepared to do so,
leaving the rest of the loads behind in charge of
Dr. T. in the hope that, on finding some of their
companions gone, the rest would collect and follow.
The experiment proved a success, and we were able
to reunite our forces about three-quarters of a mile
outside Likoro.   Soon after this a horseman appeared
who professed to have come as a messenger from the
king of Kano to salute us and bid us welcome to his
city.   After marching about eight miles we halted
for the night at a place called Kwatakori. The water
which we obtained for drinking here was, I think, the
very worst we were reduced to using during the whole
of our journey.   To quote the words of the diary it
looked " as though it had been used for washing
very dirty clothes and had then passed through a
sewer." A former inhabitant of the fen country in
England, on settling in London, is said to have
written to a friend whom he had left behind, complaining of the water which he was compelled to
drink, because it possessed neither taste, smell nor
colour.   There were comparatively few occasions
during the course of our recent journey when a
complaint such as this could with any justice have
been made ; in all too many instances the three
characteristics above mentioned were present to-

OUR RESIDENCE IN KANO, ENTRANCE PORCH OPPOSITE TO THE LEFT.

[To face page 99.

gether. Considering the fact that the Hausas drink as a rule nothing but water, and never attempt either to strain or filter it, it is surprising that diseases caused by impure water are not of universal occurrence. After a march of seven days, during which, troubles with our carriers, which it would only weary the reader to narrate, were of constant occurrence, we arrived at a place called Keffi, within ten miles of the town of Kano. During the course of the evening which we spent here, a messenger from the king of Kano arrived, bringing with him as a preliminary present twenty thousand cowries, a goat, a large jar of honey and a small sack of bread. Not having tasted any bread for upwards of three months, we lost no time in testing its quality, nor was the relish with which we ate it destroyed by the fact that a large amount of red pepper had been employed in its manufacture. The messenger from the king took care to inform us that his majesty regarded us as by far the most important visitors who had as yet visited Kano! This was, of course, simply intended as a hint as to the value of the present it would be suitable for us to give.

From Zaria to Kano the level of the country gradually declines, the latter place being nearly a thousand feet lower than the former. The exact height of Kano, according to our calculations, is 1425 feet above sea-level. The country, which is

for the most part thinly wooded, begins to show, as
one approaches Kano, increasing signs of cultivation.
Within three days' march of the city, we saw for the
first time since leaving Loko single houses attached
to farms and away from the protection of any
fortified village or town. On December 23, eight
days after leaving Zaria, we arrived outside Kano,
and entered the city by one of its southern gates.
The name of Kano had been sounding in our ears
so constantly for upwards of a year past that it was
with feelings of considerable curiosity not unmixed
with thankfulness for our safe arrival, that we
entered at length this great metropolis of the Soudan.
The walls of the town are from twenty to forty feet
in height, and as much as fifteen miles in circumference. They are built of hardened mud, and if
kept in good repair, as is at present the case, would
form a splendid protection against any native attack.
A considerable portion of the immense space thus
enclosed within the walls is cultivated land, the
object being to render the city independent of food
supplies from without in the event of a protracted
siege. The first house which was offered to us on
our arrival was one built in Arab style, the rooms of
which, glass windows being here unknown, were so
dark that it would have been necessary to keep a
lamp burning perpetually in them. I asked, therefore, that we might be given a house built in native

Hausa style, such being in every way more healthy and more suited to the conditions under which the people here live. We were accordingly assigned a house on the outskirts of the inhabited portion of the town, which consisted of a garden or courtyard, covering about an acre of land, and two mud-built rooms with a conical thatch roof. Soon after our arrival, a supplementary present from the king appeared consisting of a hundred thousand cowries, an ox, a goat, three immense sacks of rice and a large bag of wheat. On receiving the cowries I was informed, what I subsequently ascertained to be correct, that it was customary to give the bearer of the present ten thousand cowries for himself. They are delivered as a rule in bags containing twenty thousand each. Noticing that the man who was responsible for their safe carriage had brought one which was obviously underweight, some two thousand cowries having been extracted from it, I asked him if he was certain that this particular bag contained its proper amount. On receiving his assurance to this effect, I told him to sit down and count from this bag the ten thousand cowries, which, according to native custom, I owed him. He did so with great alacrity, thinking, no doubt, that the white man was sadly lacking in sagacity to allow a creditor to count his own money unchecked. I noticed that he took full advantage of his privilege, and, so far as I could judge, the sum which he counted exceeded by at least two thousand cowries that to which he was entitled. His task completed, I asked him again if he was sure that the bag as delivered by him had originally contained twenty thousand cowries. On his replying in the affirmative, I suggested to him that this being so, the amount which remained over must therefore be ten thousand. On his assuring me that my calculation was correct, I told him to leave with me the ten thousand which he had just counted and to take the rest as his due. He departed with a look of chagrin upon his face which it was piteous to see, but doubtless with his opinion as to the intelligence of the white man very considerably improved.

On Christmas Day, two days after our arrival in the town, we went to pay our respects to the king, and to offer a suitable present in return for what he had sent. Our present consisted of a large red and gold mat, a beautifully worked blue silk coverlet, a roll of silk cloth, two silk turbans, a musical box, gong, clock, a silver-topped bottle of eau de Cologne, and several other smaller articles. The palace in which the king lives is an imposing set of buildings covering many acres of land. It is built almost entirely of hardened mud, but this is so well prepared and its surface made so smooth that the effect produced is much better than might have been expected. On entering the principal porch we came into a sort of courtyard where two or three hundred people were sitting about in groups. We were then taken into a building in which we were kept waiting for two hours, while our present was being submitted to the king for inspection. When at length admitted into the audience chamber, it proved to be so dark that we could with difficulty make out the form of the king reclining on a raised platform about thirty feet away from where we stood. His face was so covered up that nothing but his eyes remained visible. Our conversation consisted almost entirely of mutual salutations; he saluted us, we saluted him; he saluted us much, we saluted him much; he saluted us very much, we saluted him very much; and this went on gradually increasing in vigour of expression for some considerable time. He then made an ineffectual attempt to pronounce my name, but only succeeded in saying Rubshi. Lastly he enquired if we were traders, and then told us that we might retire, which we proceeded to do amidst general salutations from some fifty courtiers who had been present at the interview. On returning to our house the Maji, the king's chief executive minister, sent to ask for a present in return for the one which he had given us, also for a present for his son for having brought it to us. The value of his present had been about seven shillings. I sent him one worth about three pounds, together with one for his son of the

value of fifteen shillings. He returned the latter
as not being sufficiently good. As it was absolutely
necessary to conciliate his good will in view of
our staying for some time in the town, I added
largely to it and sent it back again. He then sent
a message of thanks saying that we had shown that
we properly understood the customs of the Hausa
people.

So ended the Christmas Day which we spent in
Kano. As we tried to join in spirit with the many
friends who we knew would be remembering us then
at home, we could not but long that the time might
soon come when the " good tidings of great joy "
proclaimed on the first Christmas morning might be
brought within the reach of the inhabitants of this
great city.

In the following chapter I hope to give a general
description of the town and more especially of its
market. I would close this present chapter with a
few incidents of interest extracted from the diary.

December 29.—A messenger has arrived from the
Maji with a musical box, which some previous
traveller had presented to the king, and which we
were requested to mend. He was followed by a man
bringing a watch which he said had been given to
him by Captain Monteuil, the hair-spring of which
was gone. We brought the concentrated essence of
our triple wisdom to bear on the musical box, and

succeeded at length in discovering what was the matter, but were unable to advance any further. Dr. T. went to the palace this morning, and sold to the Maji on behalf of the king some rolls of silk for which we are to receive rather more than three quarters of a million cowries. Despatched to-day a special messenger with letters for England *viâ* Lokoja.

December 31.—Made arrangements with a very intelligent-looking Mallam to come here daily as my teacher. His name is Abd el Kadr. I am to pay him four thousand cowries a week for his services.

January 6, 1895.—There are immense quantities of flying foxes here. Towards evening they may often be seen flying in long regular lines with a steady flight, quite different from bats.

January 15.—According to my Mallam Abd el Kadr and Baba, the latter of whom is a native agent of the Royal Niger Company, the annual tributes paid by the various States to Sokoto are as follows :—Kano sends 100 horses, 15,000 tobes of various patterns, 10,000 turbans, and several other miscellaneous articles. Katsena sends 100 slaves, besides horses and cowries ; Garim Bautshi 500 slaves, and Adamawa 10,000. (According to another account which I subsequently received this should be reduced to 2,000.)

January 18.—An Arab offered to-day to lend me

money in exchange for a cheque to be cashed in Tripoli. He would, I presume, require at least a hundred per cent. for so doing, but it is interesting to ascertain the possibility of borrowing money in Central Africa.

January 19.—Have just completed the operation of baking bread, which I had undertaken to-day in consequence of Bonner being ill. Had it not been that an internal convulsion of some unknown character had seriously affected the baking possibilities of our oven, and had there not been something wrong with the flour, and lastly, had not a considerable portion of the exterior clay adjacent to the oven collapsed, and rendered necessary a modified building operation while the bread was still in course of baking, it would no doubt have been a conspicuous success. As it is, I have come to the definite conclusion that in the event of our safe return to England, I will not attempt to injure the trade of the existing bakers by setting up as their rival. This is the first time I have tried to bake bread, though I have made several previous attempts at cake-making. One such in Tunis was attended with very untoward results. After duly studying what professed to be a guide to cookery, I constructed a cake out of the materials suggested, with one or two slight changes, or rather improvements. Something, however, went wrong with the operation. The cake having apparently subsided, instead of rising, as the cookery-book said it should have done, when the operation of baking was at length complete, its weight suggested a suspicion that it had become prematurely fossilized. Feeling, as I did, that it would be most unbecoming to keep for one's own use a cake of so unique a character, in the kindness of my heart but at the same time with most reprehensible carelessness as to probable results, I presented it to our native servant. Next morning he with difficulty dragged himself as far as our house, to tell us that he was sorry to say that he felt quite unequal to doing any of our work, and that he must return home at once to recruit.

January 21.—Bonner has just developed an attack of dysentery ; Salam, our Arab boy, is also very unwell. According to a set of observations which I have taken, the longitude of Kano is 8° 29' 15" east ; our time is therefore thirty-three minutes fifty-seven seconds fast of Greenwich.

January 26.—Completed my ride round the outside of the walls to-day. There are in all thirteen gates in addition to a watergate to let out floods. On the N.E. of the city there are several swamps outside the walls. The walls themselves are a good deal out of repair on this side ; evidently no attack is expected from this direction.

February 8.—Salam very nearly succumbed to-day

to a most sudden and violent attack of black-water fever. At 2 A.M. he complained of feeling very unwell, and by 6 A.M. his temperature had risen to 105°, but after this he seemed distinctly to improve. At 1 P.M., however, he suddenly collapsed, his pulse stopped beating, his breathing became imperceptible, and he was cyanosed and suffering from extreme cold. Dr. T. injected brandy and subsequently quinine, placed large mustard poultices on his legs and back, and a hot-water bottle at his feet, with the result that in about half an hour he began to show signs of coming round. By 8 P.M. he was out of any immediate danger.

February 9.—Bonner developed black-water fever this morning. I am beginning reluctantly to alter my opinion as to the potential healthiness of Kano. Two days' more work should bring to an end my revision of the dictionary ; I began letter Z this morning. Dr. T. went to the Maji to-day to say that I had decided to leave Kano shortly, and to ask for the payment of four hundred thousand cowries which are still owing. He was very civil, promised to pay within two days, and offered to come round to see our sick patients, as he had some medicine which he said would do them good.

The difficulty just alluded to of obtaining payment for goods sold to a king was one of constant occurrence at the various places at which we stopped. The king was usually willing to pay thirty per cent. more than anyone else, but this advantage, as far as we were concerned, was often more than outweighted by the difficulty of extracting from him or his representative the amount agreed upon. In Kano the excuses invented for delaying payment would have been amusing had they not at the same time caused us really serious inconvenience. If, for example, after waiting several weeks we sent a polite message to the Maji to say that we were in need of money and desired to be paid at once, he would say, "*Sai jibi,*" *i.e.,* "It shall be paid the day after to-morrow." If, after waiting three or four days more, we sent again, he would say, "*Sai gobe,*" "It shall be paid to-morrow." If we sent to receive it on the following day, he would take care to be out; if at home, a message would come out to say that he had been taken suddenly ill, and was not fit to see any visitors or to answer any questions; if caught in the very act of going out, he would say, it shall be paid that very evening; if we sent again in the evening, a message would come to say, that he had gone out to eat with somebody else, and could not therefore attend to business. If eventually found in, say next morning, he would say that he had ordered the money to be got ready but that some mistake had occurred. He would even try to give an air of plausibility to his lies by a piece of acting : thus he would call up one of his servants and tell him in our hearing to go and fetch the money at once. The man would stay away until our messenger, whom we had left to bring the cowries, had grown tired of waiting, who would then be told that if he would only be good enough to go away, the money would be sent after him immediately. In this way we were kept waiting for part of the money due to us for very nearly three months.

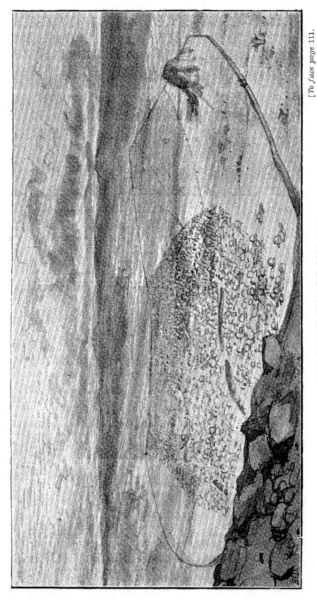

[*To face page* 111.

VIEW OF KANO FROM THE DALA HILL.

The Goron Duchi hill appears on the right about three miles off. Twelve miles of the wall of the city are shown. The two pools in the centre of the inhabited portion are the Jakhara.

CHAPTER VIII.

KANO.

How many of those whose knowledge of geography is
by no means below the average would nevertheless find
a difficulty in giving an immediate answer if asked to
say in which of the five continents the town of Kano
was situated! And yet London is probably not more
generally known throughout the continent of Europe
than is Kano throughout an equal area in the Central
Soudan. It would be difficult to find an inhabitant
of even an obscure village, within several hundred
miles of Kano, who could not tell you something of
this great commercial capital of Hausaland, and who,
if he had not been there himself, had not at least
conversed with traders who had come from it. The
market of Kano is the most important in the whole
of tropical Africa, and its manufactures are to be
met with from the Gulf of Guinea on the south to
the Mediterranean on the north, and from the Atlantic
on the west to the Nile, or even the Red Sea, on the
east. The stranger, who in conversation with a
native expresses an interest in any town or place

at which he may be staying in the Central Soudan,
is constantly liable to be interrupted by the remark,
" You have not yet seen Kano." Just as in London
we might hope to come across any English friend
whom we had for years lost sight of and whose where-
abouts were unknown, so to Kano one would naturally
go in order to find any native of the Central Soudan
of whose movements all definite trace had been lost.
It is the great meeting-point, not only for Hausas
but for other races far and near. Monteuil gives
it as his opinion that no less than two million people
pass through the city in the course of each year.
The Tuarek of the desert comes in touch here with
the natives of Adamawa and the south ; the Arab
merchant meets here with traders from Lake Tchad,
on the one side, and the Niger or even the Atlantic
sea-board, on the other. Here, too, are to be found
Mussulman pilgrims from far and near on their way
to or from Mecca. Of the actual population of the
town we found it extremely difficult to form any
satisfactory estimate. It was impossible to count
the houses in the town, or to calculate the average
number of inhabitants which each contained. The
nearest approximation to a satisfactory estimate that
we obtained was by a deduction from the average
daily death-rate. I was assured by a Mallam, whose
occupation largely consisted in chanting songs over
the dead, that the average number of funerals *per*

diem was ten. Assuming this statement to be correct and the average length of human life in Kano to be thirty years, this would give a population of rather over one hundred thousand. The slaves in Kano would probably constitute considerably more than half of the whole population, though here again it was impossible to secure any definite statistics.

The importance of the town is due, first, to the native industries which it contains ; and secondly, to the trade which is centred here largely in consequence of the existence of these industries. They consist chiefly of the weaving of cloth from native-grown cotton, and in the making and dyeing of various articles of clothing therefrom. It would be well within the mark to say that Kano clothes more than half the population of the Central Soudan, and any European traveller who will take the trouble to ask for it, will find no difficulty in purchasing Kano-made cloth at towns on the coast as widely separated from one another as Alexandria, Tripoli, Tunis or Lagos. The cloth is, woven on narrow looms, the separate strips being never more than four inches in width. These are sewn together so neatly that no join could be detected except by very careful investigation. By far the greater part of the cloth is dyed blue, the native indigo, which grows wild all over the country, being used for this purpose. There is also a scarlet dye very commonly used for dyeing

articles of clothing.   Nearly half a century ago
Dr. Barth wrote in reference to this export trade
from Kano, " In taking a general view of the subject,
I think myself justified in estimating the whole produce of this manufacture, as far as it is sold abroad,
at the very least at about three hundred millions ;
and how great this national wealth is will be understood by my readers when they know that from fifty
to sixty thousand cowries, or from four to five pounds
sterling a year, a whole family may live in that
country with ease, including every expense, even
that of clothing." Another native industry consists
in the tanning of leather, goat-skins being those
most commonly used.   These skins, after being
exceedingly well tanned, are dyed red, and are exported far and wide throughout the Soudan.   Large
quantities of them are used in Kano in the manufacture of shoes and sandals, Kano sandals being
only second to Kano cloth as an article of export.

To pass on, then, to the import trade of Kano,
there is one article scarcely known even by name
in Europe, which far and away surpasses in importance every other article of commerce throughout the whole of the Western and Central Soudan.
Though not found originally in any part of the
Hausa States, there is nevertheless no village or
hamlet, however small or remote, in which it is not
constantly used.   The article to which I refer is the

kola-nut. It is the product of a tree called " Sterculia acuminata," which is found in greatest perfection
in the country to the back of the Gold Coast Colony.
It is also found as far east as the river Gambia, and,
with more or less frequency, in all the intervening
country. The fruit resembles a large-sized chestnut,
and is encased in long pods, each containing four

KOLA-NUTS (*Sterculia acuminata*).

to six nuts. It grows like chestnuts, in bunches
of three or four on the tree. Round the kola-nut
there is usually a black line, sometimes two, at which
it can be divided or subdivided. The colour is
generally brick-red, though in some countries, especially in the far west, there are all sorts of intermediate
shades between red and white. In the country of
the Bambarra tribe the kola-nut plays an important

part in private and public life ; the colour in this
case has a special significance : a white kola is always
a sign of friendship and hospitality; proposals of marriage, acceptances or refusals, defiances, declarations of
war, etc., are conveyed by the sending of a number of
kolas of the prescribed colour.   The kola from Gandja,
which is of a uniformly red colour, is the one most
frequently brought to Kano, as it keeps better than
any other.   The most minute care and attention on
the part of the merchant is necessary in order that
the kolas may reach the market in good saleable condition.   They are carried for the most part in Kano-
made baskets, each of which contains three or four
thousand kolas, while two of them form a donkey-
load.   If treated with the utmost care, the nuts may
be preserved fresh two or even three years, but in
order to secure this they must be kept constantly
damp.   If exposed to the air and allowed to dry, the
kola opens along the black line mentioned above,
wrinkles, and becomes as hard as wood.   In this
condition it has lost ninety per cent. of its value.
During the march the nuts are packed in baskets and
covered with fresh green leaves.   Every four or five
days they ought to be re-packed, in order that the
leaves may be renewed, and that the nuts which are
touched with mildew may be removed.   The large
profits obtainable on the sale of those which reach
the various markets in good condition compensate

for the risk and trouble of their carriage. At Gandja the average nut costs five cowries; at Say, on the middle Niger, seventy to eighty; at Sokoto, a hundred; at Kano, a hundred and forty to two hundred and fifty; at Kuka, on Lake Tchad, two hundred and fifty to three hundred.

What, then, one may naturally ask, are the peculiar virtues of this fruit, which forms by far the most important article of commerce in the Central Soudan? The fact that for generations past it has been eagerly sought after by rich and poor alike, and that men will constantly spend the last cowries they possess in buying one to chew, seems clearly to show that it is something more than a mere luxury. The scientific analysis of the nut shows the existence of a large quantity of tannin and of an alkaloid analogous to théine and caféine. The natives believe that it keeps off the pangs of hunger and enables them to work for long periods without food. As a stimulant it takes the place which tea and coffee occupy with us, both of these being here practically unknown. Owing to its extremely bitter and unpleasant taste we were prevented from giving the sustaining properties of the kola a fair trial. On the occasions when, through lack of food, we would gladly have made the experiment, we were unable to obtain the nut. Whatever its real virtues may be, it is certain that the commercial power of Kano is to a very large extent dependent upon the millions of kolas which its market contains.*

The next most important article of commerce imported into Kano is probably salt. No salt is found throughout the whole of the Hausa States. The parts of the country which lie within a hundred and fifty miles of the rivers Niger and Binué are for the most part supplied with English salt imported by the Royal Niger Company. Kano and the central districts are dependent upon native salt brought upon camels across the southern portion of the Great Sahara, i.e., from Asben and Bilma. The price of salt, as sold by retail in the Kano market, is about one shilling per pound, being very nearly equal to that of sugar which is imported from Egypt viâ Tripoli. Dr. Barth travelled for some distance in company with a salt caravan consisting of no less than three thousand camels. There are also on sale swords, spears, and many other articles made of native-wrought iron. The article desired is first formed in wax, and from this a clay mould is made into which the molten iron can be poured. Owing to their inability to manufacture steel, the Hausas find great difficulty in making satisfactory files, and one or two of these which we had

* For several of the above details in regard to the kola-nut I am indebted to Colonel Monteil's recently published ' St. Louis a Tripoli par le Tchad.'

brought with us were gladly bought by native blacksmiths.

Of the European goods in the market, by far the greater part have come across the desert from the Mediterranean. The caravans which come from the north bring about twelve thousand camel-loads of goods annually, consisting of copper chiefly in the form of manufactured articles, sugar, pepper, gunpowder, needles, cloves, white cloth turbans, red silk burnouses, Arab woollen dresses, red Soudanese caps, mirrors, red coral beads, etc. The time occupied between Kano and Tripoli varies from three to nine months, the distance being about eighteen hundred miles. There are two distinct routes by which the desert may be crossed—the one leading directly north from Kano *viâ* Zinder, Asben and Ghat; the other leading from Kuka on Lake Tchad *viâ* Bilma and Murzuk. On leaving England it was my intention to return from Kano by way of the Great Sahara to Tripoli, as it seemed likely that this would prove a more healthy route than that which we were compelled to follow on the way out. On making inquiries at Kano as to the route *viâ* Zinder and Asben, we were informed that the Tuareks, through whose territory it would be necessary to pass, were so hostile to Europeans that it would be quite impossible for any man to go this way. Several Arabs, we were told, had recently been murdered by them because, owing to their light complexion, the Tuareks believed them to be Christians in disguise, and this, notwithstanding their protestation of being orthodox Mussulmans.

Finding this route closed, we turned our attention to the other, *viâ* Lake Tchad and Bilma. We found, however, to our great disappointment, that this was even more effectually closed than the former. For nearly two years past all trade between Kano and the lake has been suspended in consequence of the civil war, which has long been raging in the province of Bornou. Soon after the capture of Khartoum and the death of Gordon, a man named Rabbah, an ex-slave of Zubehr Pasha, was sent by the Mahdi to act as governor of the province of Darfur. After a time, fearing lest he should become too powerful, the Mahdi recalled him to Omdurman. Rabbah, suspecting that the Mahdi intended to kill him, refused to obey his summons, and instead of returning to Omdurman began to march towards the west with a considerable army of devoted followers, whom he had collected around him in Darfur. He invaded and subjugated the two provinces of Wadai and Baghirmi, and eventually attacked the Sultan of Bornou. A battle, or rather a succession of battles, was fought, as the result of which Rabbah gained possession of Kuka, the capital, a town of sixty thousand inhabitants, which he utterly destroyed.

At the time of our residence in Kano, he was reported to be in Khadeijah, a town to the north-east of Kano, between it and Lake Tchad. It would have been impossible to find a single carrier or servant willing to attempt the journey to Lake

NATIVE BASKET WOVEN WITH GRASS OF SEVERAL DIFFERENT COLOURS.

Tchad under existing circumstances, and to travel without native servants was of course impossible. For a short time it seemed as though it might prove possible to combine the two desert routes by going north as far as Zinder, and then crossing by a little-used track to Bilma, which lies on the direct road

from Lake Tchad to Tripoli. On further inquiry, however, we found that the route from Zinder to Bilma,
a distance of about five hundred miles, lay across an
almost waterless desert, the wells being in at least one
instance ten days' march from one another. As a
camel, under the most favourable circumstances, can
with difficulty exist for ten days without a drink, and
as, moreover, we were informed that the tribes fre-
quenting the earlier portion of this route were of an exceedingly treacherous and hostile disposition, we were
reluctantly forced to abandon this too as impracticable.

To return to the articles of merchandise in the
Kano market : there are usually on sale, either in the
market or in the houses of merchants, ivory, ostrich
feathers, natron, camels, horses, donkeys, and cattle.
The ivory is imported chiefly from Adamawa. A
considerable quantity is always to be had, though it
is seldom brought into the market for sale. Ostrich
feathers also in large quantities are to be obtained
by private negotiation ; most of these are exported
to Tripoli. Camels are used for the trade which goes
north from Kano, horses and donkeys for that which
goes south, though during the rainy season these are
of little or no use.

Bread is on sale in the market for about half the
year ; it is made in the form of buns and mixed with
a distressingly large quantity of pepper. The wheat
from which it is made is grown in the districts which

HAUSA SHOES MADE OF RED LEATHER CARVED WOODEN SPOON, AND WOODEN AMULET.

[To face page 122.

lie a little to the north of the town of Kano. Buying
and selling in the market is scarcely ever carried on
without the intervention of a third person, who acts
as a sort of broker and receives from the seller five
per cent. of the price agreed upon. Even when a
bargain is made outside the market, some third
person invariably turns up in order to claim this fee.
If the sale be effected in a private house, the five
per cent. is paid to the master of the house. Buying
and selling, where Arabs or natives are concerned,
is a far more tedious operation than can easily be
explained. If the article in question be of any
considerable value, the purchase or sale, as the case
may be, is often a work not merely of hours but of
days. When travelling to the north of the Sahara
Desert, as described in Chapter II., my companion
and I were anxious on one occasion to dispose of two
camels, for which we had no further use. The camels
were in very good condition and had no visible
defects of any kind. Two Arabs who were desirous
of becoming purchasers, came to us and said that, as
a result of a careful examination of our camels, they
had discovered that they were both suffering from
almost every disease to which a camel is liable, and
would soon become absolutely useless to their owners,
but that nevertheless they were willing to purchase
them, naming a price which was about a quarter of
their actual value. We replied by pointing out

several unique virtues that the camels possessed, which would render them quite invaluable to any purchaser, offering at the same time to sell them for about six times the amount which they had named. The Arabs withdrew with an expression of horror and contempt, but in about half an hour came back to say that they had discovered one or two further deficiencies which our camels possessed, but that, this discovery notwithstanding, they were willing to make some considerable advance upon their original offer. We replied by pointing out one or two further merits on the part of the camels which we had before omitted to mention, but said that despite this fresh discovery, we were willing to accept a somewhat lower price than that which we had at first asked. Negotiations of this kind had to be carried on for no less than three days before we succeeded in selling the camels at a reasonable price. The above is a very fair illustration of the trouble and waste of time connected with buying and selling where either Arabs or natives are concerned.

The last article of commerce deserving of mention, and to which fuller reference will be made in a subsequent chapter, is slaves. There are usually about five hundred slaves at a time on sale in Kano market, and they are bartered for and sold in just the same way as other merchandise. According to Dr. Barth, whose testimony was unhappily confirmed by our own experience, Kano is far from being a place to be recommended as a health resort. Its height above the sea, which, according to our calculations was 1425 feet, ought to insure its being free from the malaria, which has given so ill a reputation to the low-lying districts along the bed of the Niger Such freedom it is, however, very far indeed from possessing. Its unhealthiness is probably due to the large quantity of stagnant water to be found within the city. Into one large pool, called the Jekara, all the offal and refuse from the market is being constantly thrown, whilst the drinking water for the immediate neighbourhood, if not taken from the pool itself, is taken from wells sunk in suspicious proximity to it. The hollows in which the water lies have for the most part been made by the excavation of mud for building purposes in time past. They are usually covered by a floating water plant, " Pistia stratiotes." By the time that the wet season commences many of them have disappeared altogether. There are a certain number of wells on the outskirts of the inhabited portion of the town, one of which we were fortunate enough to possess within our own courtyard, from which very tolerable water could be obtained. The natives suffer from drinking impure water, though to a less extent than might naturally have been imagined. Dr. Tonkin was of opinion that the severe attack of dysentery from which both he and Mr. Bonner suffered, was caused by eating some native butter which had been washed in the water of the market. During the latter part of our stay in Kano we always took the precaution of boiling all the butter before eating it. The unhealthiness of Kano, however, as compared with that of other Hausa towns, is almost entirely due to causes which are removable. If many of the stagnant pools were filled in, and the most elementary precautions adopted to prevent the pollution of the others, and improve the drainage of the town, there is no reason whatever why Europeans should not live here in comparative comfort and health. One can only hope that the time will soon come when it will be possible to make an experiment in this direction.

CHAPTER IX.

SLAVERY AND SLAVE-RAIDING.

ONE out of every three hundred persons now living in the world is a Hausa-speaking slave. This statement sounds so utterly monstrous and incredible that the reader, whose acquaintance with the Central Soudan is but small, may well be excused if he hesitate to accept it without definite evidence as to its truth. It is generally admitted that the Hausa-speaking population number at least fifteen million, *i.e.*, roughly speaking, one per cent. of the world's population. Colonel Monteil, who has recently travelled through a considerable portion of the Hausa States, gives it as his opinion that the slave population is far in excess of the free. Though this estimate appears to me too high, it is I think a fact which admits of no doubt whatever, that at the very least one-third are in a state of slavery, or, in other words, that one out of every three hundred of the world's population is a Hausa-speaking slave. Slave-raiding and the traffic in slaves, to which it ministers, is the great overshadowing evil of the

Central Soudan. There is no tract of equal size in
Africa, or indeed in the world, where the slave trade
at the present moment flourishes so largely and so
entirely unchecked by any European influence. So
much has been said and written about the slave
trade of East Africa, that it is certainly somewhat
disheartening to learn that, bad as matters are on
the East Coast, they are immeasurably worse on the
West. To make the case still more distressing from
an English standpoint, the whole of the country
where this slavery and slave-raiding is flourishing so
luxuriantly, is British territory, or if this expression
be objected to as premature, is within the British
"sphere of influence," having been definitely recognised as such by the treaty of Berlin. By claiming for
ourselves this vast tract of country we have claimed
one of the most important and most valuable sections
of equatorial Africa, but we have at the same time
claimed for ourselves a great responsibility, from
which we cannot, if we would, set ourselves free.
The great majority of the slaves in Hausaland are
obtained, not from foreign or outside sources, but
from villages and towns the inhabitants of which are
of the same tribe and race as their captors. The
practical result of this is that the country is subject
to nearly all the evils of perpetual civil war. There
is no real security for life or property anywhere. At
any moment the king, in whose territory any town

or village lies, may receive a message from the king
to whom he is himself tributary, ordering him to
send at once a given number of slaves on pain of
having his own town raided. He thereupon selects
some place within his own territory, and without,
perhaps, the shadow of an excuse, proceeds to attack
it and to carry off its inhabitants as slaves. The
attack is usually made in overwhelming numbers,
so as to prevent any serious resistance. Any who
attempt to resist are massacred on the spot, the rest
are made to march in fetters to the town of their
captors, whence they are either passed on to some
central slave market to be sold, or kept for awhile in
order to be included in the annual tribute payable to
the Sultan of Sokoto. Anyone who reads the ' Auto-
biography of a Slave,' by Mr. H. H. Johnson, who
was formerly a Consul on the West coast, and is now
Commissioner of Nyassaland, will gain a most real-
istic idea of the sufferings entailed by slavery as at
present carried on in Hausaland. Moreover, the evils
resulting from slavery should by no means be regarded simply from the point of view of the person
enslaved. As I walked through one slave market
after another in the various Hausa towns, it often
seemed to me that the persons most injured, *i.e.,*
most degraded by the slave trade, were not the
slaves but the slave-owners. If the latter only had
to be considered, it would still behove everyone

who cared anything for the development of the
African native, to use his utmost endeavour to
remove what is at present an insuperable obstacle
to his advance.

During the course of our march from Loko to
Egga, *viâ* Kano, a distance of about eight hundred
miles, we had frequent opportunities of observing the
general insecurity of life and property which the
existence of the slave trade produces. Soon after
leaving Loko we entered the town of Nassarawa,
where we were compelled to wait till the return of its
king from a slave raid, on which he was then absent.
On reaching Jimbambororo, a village a few miles
further on, we were told that its king was not
"feeling sweet," owing to the fact that twenty of his
subjects had that very morning been seized as slaves
by the people of an adjacent town. On leaving this
village we passed a spot where two days before
fifteen native merchants had been carried off as
slaves; and again, shortly before reaching· Katchia,
we were shown another point on our path where,
within the previous two days, a similar fate had
befallen five other travellers. On arriving at the
large town of Zaria, in the market place of which we
saw about two hundred slaves exposed for sale, we
were once again informed that the king was absent
on a slave-raiding expedition. During our stay in
Kano about a thousand slaves were brought into the

town on a single occasion as the result of such an expedition. In the course of our march from Kano to Bida we passed towns and villages, literally without number, which had been recently destroyed and their inhabitants sold as slaves ; and this, as has been already explained, not by any foreign invader, but by the king in whose territory the places themselves were situated.

Slaves form to a great extent the currency of the country, where larger amounts are involved than can be conveniently paid in cowries. When, for instance, a native is about to travel for any considerable distance, he will usually take with him slaves proportionate in number to the length of his proposed journey. After travelling perhaps a hundred miles he will stop and sell one of his slaves, and with the proceeds will travel another hundred miles when he will sell a second. He will probably so arrange that, by the time he gets home again, he will have sold all the slaves which he took with him on setting out, with the exception of his personal attendants.

The prices of slaves differ largely according to age, sex, and the scarcity or abundance at the particular time and place at which they are sold. In Kano the maximum price, which, reducing the cowries to English money, would be from seven to ten pounds, is paid for a girl aged about fourteen. A young man of eighteen years would fetch about six pounds, a man of thirty about four, the price then decreasing as the age increases.

The following are the customs which I ascertained to exist in Kano in regard to the marriage of slaves. A freeman may not marry a slave nor *vice versâ* ; if a freeman begets a child by a slave who is his own property, he may not afterwards sell her. In the event of two slaves wishing to marry, they may do so with the consent of their respective masters ; in this case the first child is regarded as belonging to the owner of the woman, the second to the owner of the man, and so on alternately. A master is at liberty to maltreat his slave to an unlimited extent short of actually killing him. If, as not unfrequently happens, a master has no work for his slaves to do, it is customary for him to turn them adrift to provide for themselves ; in this case they have to pay a sort of monthly tax to their master of three thousand cowries. To raise this amount, in addition to that required for the purchase of food, is often a work of very great difficulty.

In regard to the general treatment to which the average slave is exposed at the hand of his master, I found it exceedingly difficult to form any satisfactory opinion. There are undoubtedly many cases in which, so far as material comfort is concerned, the slave is every bit as well off as if he had remained free. On the other hand it is impossible to ignore the fact that a vast amount of cruelty is practised not only in the capture, but in the after-treatment of many, if not actually of a majority, of the slaves. Moreover, the very fact that so many slaves appear contented with their position and seem to have but little desire to rise above it, is itself a strong argument against the continuance of slavery, for is not this very contentment a proof of the degradation to which the slave has been reduced, inasmuch as he has ceased to aspire to a condition of freedom which is the birthright of his humanity? In many parts of the Hausa States the slaves are sufficiently numerous in proportion to the free population to overthrow the existing government and gain their freedom by force of arms, but instances of such revolutions have been exceedingly rare in the past history of the Hausas, and it is most unlikely that any attempt on a large scale to secure their freedom in this way would be successful. A considerable number of slaves are taken annually across the desert by the caravans that go to Tripoli and Tunis. On arriving at either of these places they are supposed by the existing laws to become free, but in the former, and probably to a less extent in the latter, there are many who either through ignorance or fear are prevented from claiming the privileges to which they are entitled.

The chance of a slave being able to save up enough

money in his own country to buy himself free is exceedingly small, and even under favourable circumstances would require many years for its accomplishment.

In considering any suggestions for the ultimate abolition of the slave trade, which, if it come at all, must come as the result of European, or, in other words, of English intervention, it is evident that one of the most important things, which will have to be done in order to render this possible, must be the substitution of some other satisfactory currency. At the present moment slaves are used for two distinct purposes, first as currency, where any large amount such as the State tribute is involved, and secondly as carriers. No solution of the problem will be permanently satisfactory which does not take account of, and endeavour to supply in some more convenient way, these two needs. Of the tribute payable by all the Hausa States to Sokoto, at least three quarters is paid in slaves. We were informed, on what appeared credible authority, that the King of Adamawa sends annually ten thousand slaves.

Kano sends perhaps the smallest number, it is said about one hundred, the greater parts of its tribute being paid in cloth. Were slavery suddenly stopped it would be almost impossible for many of the States to find any other currency with which to pay their tribute.

Probably the best thing which could be done in order to supply this need would be to introduce in wholesale quantities the Maria Theresa dollar. This coin has for at least half a century been circulating to a limited extent, and is in some districts eagerly sought after by the natives, and though its introduction in large quantities would, for a time at any rate, reduce its purchasing value, this would ere long be

MARIA THERESA DOLLAR.

compensated for by the impetus which its use would give to trade.

There could certainly be no more philanthropic purpose to which some of the silver, of which the world has at the present time such an awkward superabundance, could be applied than the creation of a reasonable currency in this country, to replace in course of time both slaves and cowries. The latter are indeed but a caricature of what a currency

should be, lacking as they do the three characteristics which, according to political economists, a
medium of exchange should possess, namely, intrinsic
value, scarcity and portability.

The second thing necessary to be done in order to
render possible the eventual abolition of slavery is to
provide some cheaper method of carriage than that
which slave labour at present affords. I remember
once over-hearing two Welshmen arguing as to the
respective advantages of walking and going by train.
The discussion ended by the emphatic declaration on
the part of one of them to the effect than any man who
thought walking cheaper than going by train must be
a born fool. As in this case there was apparently
no question as to the carriage of luggage, I presume
the expense connected with walking to which he referred would be proportionate to the number of public-
houses which would have to be passed *en route*. The
Hausas are very far indeed from being born fools,
and once let them understand that it was cheaper to
travel otherwise than on foot, and the present system
of porterage by means of slave labour would die a
natural and immediate death. It has at last come to
be an admitted fact, as far as East Africa is concerned, that the one panacea for the slave trade still
existing there is a railway. The arguments that
have been successfully adduced for making a railway
on the East Coast, such as that to Uganda, are, with

scarcely an exception, applicable with increased force to the construction of a railway on the West Coast.

If a railway to Uganda be necessary in order to check the slave trade there, one to Kano is tenfold more necessary for the same reason. If it be necessary there in order to secure the establishment and maintenance of order, how much more is it needed here for the same objects! Lastly, if a railway to Uganda can reasonably be expected to pay a dividend, passing, as it will during a great part of its length, through districts the natural products of which are almost valueless, how much safer an investment would be offered by one which would pass through one of the most fertile and productive districts in the whole of tropical Africa. The carriage of the kola-nut from the coast to the interior would alone go far towards providing a dividend on such a railway. On one occasion I met a native caravan consisting of about a thousand men, together with a large number of donkeys, carrying kola-nuts up towards Kano. The value of the nuts in the caravan, which was only one out of several that annually come to Kano for the same purpose, was little less than a hundred thousand pounds sterling. The whole of this immense trade is at present in the hands of natives, as the course of the Niger is not such as to allow of the kolas being carried by water any part of the way.

The French regard the trade of the Central Soudan as of so great importance that they have not only talked of, but actually attempted a partial survey for, a railway which should cross the Great Sahara and connect these regions with the French provinces of Algiers and Tunis in the far north. The almost fabulous cost of such a railway will certainly prevent the realisation of this scheme, but the very fact that it has been thought worthy of serious consideration bears witness to the value which the French assign to the trade connected with these regions. The first stage in the construction of a railway to Kano would be from Lagos on the coast, to Rabbah on the river Niger. The distance from the mouth of the Niger to Rabbah is about five hundred miles; the distance, however, from Lagos to Rabbah would not be more than two hundred and sixty. The railway would probably go *via* the large Yoruba towns of Abeokuta, Ibadan, and Ilorin, and the greatest elevation which it would be necessary to cross would not be more than fourteen hundred feet. The Lagos colony is, I understand, prepared to provide, or guarantee interest on, a considerable part of the money required for the construction of this line, but is anxious to obtain some assistance from the Imperial Government before actually venturing to commence it. Near Rabbah it would be possible to build a bridge over the Niger, which would be the first step towards continuing the line into the heart of the Hausa country. From Rabbah to Kano would be about four hundred miles, the distance between Kano and Lagos by this route being almost the same as that between the Victoria Nyanza, to which the Uganda Railway is to run, and the East Coast.

The completion of a railway to Kano must however be a work of some considerable time. Meanwhile it is earnestly to be hoped that some serious effort will be made to check the slave-raiding which at present exists so universally. All that has been done up to the present to check slave-raiding has been done by the Royal Niger Company without any direct assistance from the British Government. By means of one or two small armed launches they have endeavoured to prevent slave-raiders from crossing the rivers Niger and Binué, but even were they to succeed completely in effecting this object, it would but be touching the fringe of the difficulty. A chartered company, however philanthropic a body its directors may be, cannot, without considerable assistance from the Government, attempt to cope with so stupendous an evil.

The question then suggests itself, supposing that the Government, urged on by public opinion, were prepared to make an attempt itself, or to assist the Royal Niger Company to make such, what exactly could be done to bring about the abolition of slave-raiding in this country ? Inasmuch as the obligation to contribute slaves to Sokoto as tribute necessitates the continuance of slave-raiding on the part of all the tributary states, it is obvious that the first thing to do is to bring pressure to bear upon the Sultan of Sokoto to induce him to accept native goods or produce in place of slaves and to forbid the sending of slaves to Sokoto at all. This would be the first step and a very long step towards the abolition of slave-raiding throughout the whole of the Hausa States. Its immediate effect would be to lower the commercial value of slaves and thus to decrease the inducement which tempts each petty king to raid his own towns and villages in order to raise money by the sale of their inhabitants.

It is by no means particularly likely that the Sultan of Sokoto would consent to forego his annual tribute of slaves without some considerable pressure being brought to bear upon him. Most fortunately, in view of attempting such pressure, Sokoto is far more easily accessible than Kano. There is in fact water communication the whole way to Sokoto, though, owing to the cataracts above Busa, it would be impossible to use it for purposes of continuous transport. The details connected with the exercise of this pressure would naturally be left to the Royal Niger Company, who are only waiting for further support in order to go forward in this direction.

What is wanted and what is the principal object of the publication of this book, is to enlighten public opinion as to the existence of slave-raiding and of all its attendant evils in a country for the well-being of which we have assumed the moral responsibility.

CHAPTER X.

NATIVE MEDICINES—LEPROSY, ETC.

THERE are two stalls in the Kano market not far
from one another, at one of which firewood is on sale,
and at the other medicines suitable for almost every
known or imaginary disease. The goods on sale at
the two stalls are so extraordinarily alike, that it
would require an expert to say which were intended
for firewood and which for medicine. The greater
part of the medicines used are in reality nothing but
charms. The commonest of all is a drink composed
of water which has been used to wash a piece of
board, on which a few verses of the Koran had been
previously written. I have brought back with me
a charm, the general use of which, unless its reputed
powers have been exaggerated, would cause a considerable diminution in the world's population. The
charm is to be written out in the first instance on a
board; the ink is then to be washed off. In the
mixture of water and ink thus obtained is to be
soaked a piece of wood taken from a tree that has
been struck by lightning. The mixture is then to be

used for washing the human body, the result being
that the enemy of the man who has thus washed
himself will die. Dr. Tonkin was solemnly assured
in Kano that medicine could be bought there, the
effect of which would be to turn a man into a crow
or raven. On our proceeding to make further
inquiries in view of facilitating our return to Europe
by this means, we were told that for some unexplained reason this particular medicine was not to be
had at that time. We took with us a very large
supply of English medicines, many of which we
found it quite impossible to use with any effect,
owing to the reluctance of the patients to submit to
any lengthy course of treatment. They seemed to
think that it could only be due to the incapacity of
the doctor if a disease of many years' standing could
not be cured in a day. As in most instances the
applicants for medicine were unable to read, it was
necessary to give them verbal instructions as to how
their medicine was to be taken, the result being that
the patient, after forgetting the instructions which he
had received, would occasionally have recourse to an
empirical method of treatment which was not always
productive of the best results. During our stay in
Tunis, one patient returned after the lapse of several
days to complain of the medicine which had been
given to him, and on being questioned as to how he
had used it, stated that he had first drunk some of it

and then, finding its taste disagreeable, had washed
himself with the remainder, the results of either
operation proving equally unsatisfactory. On several
occasions we were applied to for medicine in cases
where the most accomplished physician would have
been at a loss how to prescribe. One evening, for
example, after a somewhat wearisome march, we
had just pitched our tent, and were looking forward
to a more than usually meagre dinner, when I was
informed that a man had arrived bringing two fowls,
one of which on examination proved to be dead, to
pay for some medicine which he hoped to obtain from
us. After accepting his fee with great alacrity, and
making arrangements for cooking the fowl which had
been brought to us alive, Dr. Tonkin went out to
inquire the particular complaint for which the
medicine was required. He returned to inform me
that the man's favourite wife had recently run away
and that he wanted us to give him some medicine
which, if drunk by himself, would cause her to run
back to him. As we were extremely desirous of
retaining the dinner that had so opportunely arrived,
Dr. Tonkin on my suggestion, informed the man that,
although we were sorry to be unable to provide the
precise medicine he had asked for, we would, if he
wished, give him some medicine that would make
him stronger to run after his wife, which would in
the end come to the same thing. Fortunately for

us, or rather for the prospects of our dinner, the man agreed to accept this proposal, and we gave him the medicine which we thought most suitable for such a purpose. On another occasion, a man in the act of setting out for a war, that is a slave raid, applied to us for medicine which should not only render him proof against the bullets of his enemies, but should cause the bullets to rebound and injure them instead of him. We were forced on this occasion to confess our inability to supply such, or any satisfactory substitute.

Despite, however, an immense amount of superstition on the subject, the knowledge which the Hausas possess in regard to the cure of certain well-known diseases is by no means so far behind our own as might have been expected. On stating to a native in Kano that we in England had been trying to discover a cure for hydrophobia, he at once replied that they, the Hausas, had long since discovered such. In the event of a man being bitten by a mad dog, the dog is immediately killed, and its liver is eaten by the man who has been bitten. The principle underlying this treatment is obviously the same as that which M. Pasteur discovered, the discovery of which has made his name so famous. I conversed with more than one native who assured me most positively that he had himself known a patient bitten by a mad dog, who had recovered as

L

the result of this treatment. Another remedy, of the genuineness of which no reasonable doubt can be entertained, and which is suggestive of the same principle, is that applied in cases of snake-bite. In the event of a man being bitten by a snake, an occurrence by no means uncommon in this part of Africa, he is at once taken to a native doctor, who inoculates him with poison extracted from another snake, the result being to render inoperative the poison of the snake which had bitten him. This cure for snake-bite is practised not only in Hausaland but all along the coast. Great efforts have been made by English doctors residing on the coast to ascertain the exact nature of the preparation which is used for inoculation, but hitherto without success. The native doctors are extremely unwilling to afford any information on the subject to Europeans. I was assured by an English Government official who had had many years' experience in the neighbourhood of Accra on the Gold Coast, that he had himself known a man bitten by a most venomous snake, who, having been seen by the native doctor an hour afterwards, was able to do his ordinary work as a porter on the following day. This, moreover, was only one of several instances which had come under his own personal observation. The Hausas have also some native remedies for fever and dysentery which are apparently productive of good results. We had, however, no opportunity of obtaining definite proof as to their value.

The most interesting work from a medical point of wiew, which we were able to do was the collection of a large number of statistics and details in regard to Central African leprosy. This disease exists to a most deplorable extent throughout the whole of the Central Soudan. We seldom stayed at a village, however small, in which, on inquiry, there did not prove to be at least one or two lepers. In Kano there are said to be no less than a thousand. Here they are regularly organised, their head man bearing the title of king of the lepers. Dr. Tonkin will, I trust, ere long publish a full account of the statistics which he spent immense time and labour in collecting. Meanwhile a short popular account of the spread of the disease in the country through which we passed will be of interest to many. We had with us, most fortunately, a copy of the Report * of the Indian Leprosy Commission of 1891, and Dr. Tonkin was thus enabled to proceed on exactly the same lines of inquiry as that adopted by the commissioners. Soon after the death of Father Damien in Hawaii, a sum of money was raised in England, part of which was spent in sending out this commission, composed of five doctors, to India, who were to report as to the possibility of checking the further spread of the

* 'Report of Leprosy Commission of India.' Calcutta, 1893.

disease in that country. Their report, issued as the result of wide and careful investigation, contains the conclusions at which they arrived and a full account of the evidence on which these were based. The conclusions themselves are of the most astonishing character, opposed as they are to popular opinion of almost all countries and all historical time.

The commissioners report, in fact, that leprosy is neither hereditary, infectious, nor, except in the rarest cases, contagious. They further state their opinion that it "is not directly originated by the use of any particular food, nor by any climatic or telluric conditions, nor by insanitary conditions," but that "in the great majority of cases it originates *de novo* from a sequence or concurrence of causes and conditions . . . related to each other in ways at present imperfectly known." A special committee appoined in England to draw up a memorandum upon this report expressed their disagreement with the statement that "leprosy in the majority of cases originates *de novo*," also with the statement that "the extent to which leprosy is propagated by contagion and inoculation is exceedingly small." This special committee, however, agreed with the conclusion arrived at by the commissioners to the effect that "leprosy is not diffused by hereditary transmission." In support of this latter statement they refer to the emigration of one hundred and sixty lepers from Norway to North

America. When, after the lapse of some years, Dr. Hansen visited the place in which they had settled, he found only seventeen of the original lepers still living, but not one of the descendants of these lepers had contracted the disease.

Dr. Tonkin examined in all about two hundred and twenty cases of leprosy taken from different parts of the country, some of which were of the mutilating and some of the tubercular form of leprosy. Though I have not with me the detailed statistics, it certainly appeared to me that in by far the greater proportion of cases examined, the origin of the disease could be explained on the supposition that leprosy was contagious, whilst a very considerable number of cases seemed to admit of no other explanation. Again and again we met with such a case as this. A healthy woman, none of whose ancestors or relations had been lepers, marries a husband who is a leper, and after living with him two or more years she contracts leprosy herself. A large number of such instances may of course be explained on the supposition that the cause of leprosy was her coming to live under exactly similar conditions to those under which her husband had caught the disease before, but even in these cases it seems at least as reasonable to suppose that the origin of the disease was due to a rational and well understood cause, such as contagion, as to suppose that it resulted from conditions at present unexplained and inexplicable.

No precautions of any kind are taken in order to separate the lepers or to prevent them mixing with the rest of the population. They are even to be seen selling food in the open market. Most of the lepers support themselves by begging and many of them earn a very comfortable living by this means. The length of time which the disease takes to bring about the death of the patient varies from a comparatively few months to thirty or even forty years. A leper moreover in a good position in life would usually live longer than one in poorer circumstances. As a rule, the natives regard leprosy as incurable, though we heard of instances in which it was claimed that a cure had been effected. As, however, many cases were brought to us, in which the patient imagined that he was a leper, though he was in reality suffering from some skin disease of a trifling character, it is probable that the cases alleged to have been cured had been of this kind.

At the tenth International Medical Congress held in Berlin, Mr. Jonathan Hutchinson stated his opinion that eating fish might very probably prove to be the cause of the spread of leprosy. The Indian Commission, however, reported decisively against this theory, partly on the ground that a considerable number of the patients examined by them denied ever having tasted fish, and partly because in a large number of specimens of fish brought from different parts of India no trace of the leprosy bacillus could be detected. One of the questions which we asked every patient who came to see us was, " Is there any article of food which you have given up eating since you became a leper ? " In quite half the cases examined the answer which we received was, " Yes, I have given up eating fish." In many instances they added some other article of diet, but the consensus of opinion in regard to fish far surpassed that in regard to anything else. On our proceeding to inquire why they had ceased to eat fish, the answer given would be that they considered fish as bad for lepers. On making further inquiries in view of ascertaining a possible connection between eating fish and leprosy, we ascertained that down on the coast where fish was extremely common, practically no leprosy existed. In the immediate neighbourhood of Lake Tchad where fish was also fairly abundant, leprosy was comparatively rare, whereas in Kano and other places where very little fish was to be had, leprosy was distressingly common. These facts, though at first sight they seem to tell against the fish hypothesis, on closer examination will be seen to support it most strongly. If leprosy is either caused or spread by eating fish it is of course bad fish, not good fish, from the eating of which the

disease is obtained. Wherever then fish is very
plentiful it would naturally be eaten whilst still fresh
and good, whereas in places such as Kano, where fish
is very scarce and has often to be brought considerable distances, it is nearly always stale and very
frequently putrid.

It is certainly very curious, supposing the hypothesis to have no foundation in fact, that the origin
of leprosy should be so generally believed to be in
some way connected with the eating of fish. According to the report of the Indian Commission, the
disease is as incurable as it has ever been held to be,
nor have they any remedies to recommend other than
of a simply palliative character. Except in the
event of his dying meanwhile of some other com-
plication, a man who has once contracted leprosy
must inevitably die of this disease. Though it is
unlikely that for many years to come any steps can
be taken to check the spread of leprosy in these
countries, statistics collected thence may none the
less prove useful in helping to throw light upon the
conditions under which it tends either to spread or to
decrease. Considering the wonderful progress made
in medical science during recent years, we can but
hope that the day is not far distant when we may be
enabled to understand and so eventually to eradicate
this of all diseases perhaps the most terrible and
mysterious.

Another curious complaint which often accompanies leprosy, though it is not at all necessarily connected with it, we found very common in Kano. It is a disease called ainhum, whereby the bone of the little toe becomes gradually absorbed, the result being that the toe becomes anæsthetic and eventually drops off. The Indian Commissioners speak of meeting with several such cases, the general rule in India being that in healthy persons the little toe was always the part attacked, whereas in lepers or in persons about to develop leprosy any toe or even finger might be affected.

The natives suffer very little from fever, though the Arabs who come to Kano as traders often die of it. I do not think that in the whole of our journey we saw a single case of smallpox or signs of its having previously attacked any one.

On the whole, the Hausas are a strong healthy race, and are very seldom ill or incapacitated for work, and that, despite the ink and other noxious mixtures that they drink in order to charm away non-existent diseases.

CHAPTER XI.

FAUNA AND FLORA.

THIS chapter is not intended to contain a scientific list of the fauna and flora of Hausaland, but simply a few notes on some of the plants and animals of the country, to which the attention of a traveller would be most naturally drawn. First, then, in regard to the food on which the great majority of the Hausa people live. The commonest food of all is what the natives call dawa, the Egyptians and natives of the east coast dhurra, and which in English is usually called guinea-corn. It is a species of millet (*Sorghum vulgare*), and is found nearly all over Africa, also in India and the West Indies. The name guinea-corn, which originated in the West Indies, is supposed to have been given to it because the seed was first brought there from the Guinea coast of Africa. It grows in Hausaland to a height of about eight or ten feet. Its leaves are sometimes thirty inches long, though not more than two inches wide in the broadest part. The flowers come out in large panni-cles, somewhat resembling those of maize, and are succeeded by very minute red seeds wrapped round in chaff, apparently in order to protect them against the birds. The grain, which is exceedingly hard, is ground between two stones, and is then made into a sort of porridge. This porridge forms the staple food of the country ; in fact, large numbers of the people eat nothing else. It has a sour, insipid taste, and we but seldom had recourse to it whenever it was possible to obtain rice or any other kind of grain. The physical strength by which the Hausas are as a rule distinguished, would, however, tend to show that it must possess some very supporting and nourishing qualities. The Hausas in fact attribute their superiority in strength, as compared with that of the coast tribes, to the fact that they eat guinea-corn, whereas the latter live almost entirely on yams. The yam, mention of which is found so constantly in books of African travel, is the root of a slender climbing plant (*Dioscorea sativa*), the stem of which is from eighteen to twenty feet in length. The roots are flat, either palmated or irregular shaped, and from six to eighteen inches in length. Its taste is something between that of a parsnip and a potato, and it is usually either boiled or fried, and then mashed up. It is extremely common all along the West Coast and in the neighbourhood of the larger rivers, but in the northern part of Hausaland is but seldom met with.

The sweet potato (*Convolvulus batatas*), called by the Hausas *dankali*, is very common throughout the whole of the country. It is a low trailing plant, its creeping stems extending six or eight feet from the central root. In shape it is like a thick parsnip, and in taste much sweeter than either a parsnip or a yam. Prior to the general use of the potato in England, large quantities of the sweet potato were imported into this country from Spain and the Canary Islands. It is supposed to be a native both of the East and West Indies and of China, in which latter country not only the roots, but the young leaves, are boiled and eaten.

Another root, called by the natives *rogo*, which bears some resemblance to cassava is also extensively cultivated for food.

In the southern part of the country plantains are grown to a very considerable extent, and form an agreeable change as an article of diet. The plantain (*Musa paradisiaca*) closely resembles a banana, though it is somewhat larger and coarser than its better-known relation. It grows on a tree fifteen or twenty feet in height, its leaves, which form a cluster at the top, being about six feet long. Of all existing food-plants, there is probably none, the cultivation of which requires so little attention, and which yields so large a return in proportion to the amount of land occupied. It has been calculated that twenty-five times as many people can subsist upon a piece of land planted with bananas or plantains as upon the same planted with wheat.

At Kano, and in the northern part of the Hausa States, there is scarcely any fruit at all to be had. Almost the only one worth eating is that of the pawpaw-tree (*Carica papaya*). It bears a red juicy fruit about the size of a small melon. The leaves of the tree are used by the natives for rendering tough meat tender. If a leaf of the tree is put into the pot in which the meat is boiling, or if prior to being boiled the meat be wrapped up in a leaf for half-an-hour, the toughest meat will become quite tender. We experimented in this way on one or two occasions, and satisfied ourselves as to the genuineness of its reputed powers.

The oil used in the country, both for cooking purposes and for illumination, is obtained from three different trees. In the neighbourhood of the Niger palm oil is chiefly used. This oil, which is known in England as train-oil, and is of a bright orange-yellow, is obtained from what is usually called the oil-palm (*Elæis guineensis*). The nuts are about the size of a pigeon's egg, and are found in clusters of from six to eight hundred, forming a head something like a huge pineapple. The oil has a very strong taste, and it takes a stranger some time to get accustomed to eating it.

Another very common oil is obtained from the
ground-nut (*Arachis hypogœa*).   It is an annual plant
of a trailing habit and yellow pea-shaped flower.   Its
pods contain from two to four small red seeds from
which the oil is extracted.   The oil is very thin, and

BAOBAB TREE (*Adansonia digitata*).

on this account is generally used by watchmakers in
England, and is exported from West Africa for this
purpose.

The third most commonly used oil is the product
of the shea-butter-tree.   This oil, which is of about

the same consistency as lard and not altogether
unlike it in taste, only becomes liquid under considerable heat. All the above are used alike
for eating and for burning in lamps. Rice is
to be had in most parts of the country, though
it is not generally used by the poorer classes,
guinea-corn being a much cheaper food. Wheat
is grown in small quantities to the north of Kano,
and would probably do equally well if planted
farther south.

The tree which usually forms the most distinctive
feature in the landscape is the baobab or monkey-
bread-tree (*Adansonia digitata*) called by the Hausas
kuka. This tree, which is a native of West Africa, is
one of the largest known anywhere, its trunk being
sometimes ninety feet in circumference. It is a slow-
growing tree, and is believed to live for an almost
incalculable length of time. It seldom grows to a
height of more than fifty feet, though its roots are
at least twice as long as the tree is high. It is very
seldom to be seen possessed of leaves, as these are
highly valued by the natives as a sort of condiment
to their food. They are said, moreover, to be useful
in attacks of fever and diarrhœa. The fruit, which
is about ten inches long and four in diameter, is of
a brownish colour, and has a pleasant acid taste.
The trunk of the tree is usually hollowed out and
has altogether a most ruinous appearance. This is,

due to the fact that it is extremely liable to be attacked by a fungus which, vegetating in the centre of the tree, gradually destroys the interior of the trunk without, however, affecting the growth or health of the tree. It is altogether one of the most curious, but at the same time, chiefly owing to its lack of foliage, one of the ugliest features of a Central African landscape.

One of the finest trees in the country, under the welcome shade of which we frequently stopped to rest, is the silk-cotton-tree (*Eriodendron bombax*). Its seeds are enveloped in long silken hairs closely resembling those of the true cotton, but the wool is incapable of manufacture, owing to the want of adhesion between the hairs, and is only employed for stuffing cushions and other like purposes. The cotton-cloth, which is manufactured so largely in Kano, is the product not of this tree but of the ordinary cotton-shrub which grows in several different parts of the country.

The tree which gives the best shade of any in Hausaland is a very large species of acacia (*Robinia pseudacacia*), called in America the locust-tree, and by the Hausas *dorowa*. It produces an edible fruit which is contained in a pod like that of a bean, but it is chiefly valued for the magnificent shade which it affords. It is quite a common sight to see a native market being held beneath its branches.

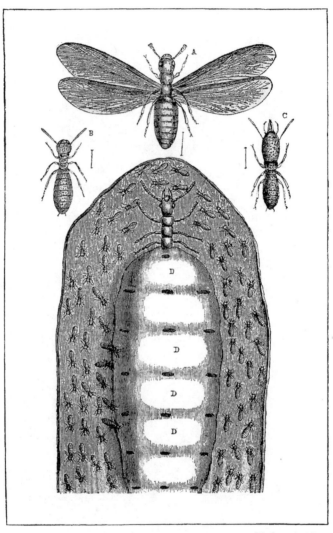

[*To face page* 161.

WHITE ANTS.

A, male   *B*, worker; *C*, soldier; *D*, fecundated female of *Termes bellicosus*, natural
size, surrounded by "workers."

Indigo grows wild in many places, and is also cultivated for the sake of the dye which it produces. It grows to a height of about two feet and bears small red flowers which are succeeded by long crooked pods containing yellow seeds. The dye is obtained by the fermentation of the leaves in water. There seems no reason why, if carefully cultivated, it should not prove a really valuable export.

Tobacco is found both in a wild and cultivated state. As, however, smoking is not practised by the natives, except to a very limited extent, its cultivation is only carried on in a few circumscribed areas.

To pass on then from the flora to the fauna of Hausaland. One of the things which will first attract the attention of the traveller is the clay-built domes rising at intervals in the forest to the height of ten or twelve feet. These are, at once, the work and the homes of what is usually known as the white ant, though in reality it has no claim to the title of ant, belonging as it does to quite a different order in the insect world, namely, that of the termites. Only the under part of these mounds is actually inhabited by the termites, the upper portion serving chiefly as a defence from the weather and to secure the necessary warmth below for the hatching of the eggs and the rearing of the young ones. The termite is at once the most destructive and the most useful of all African

M

insects. Its appetite is fairly omnivorous, its favourite
food being clothes of any kind, paper, leather and dry
wood. Its power of consuming this latter renders
almost all carpentry in Central Africa an impossibility. They are usually found in such countless
numbers that it is waste of time to attempt to
destroy them. On one occasion a number of them
commenced to emerge from a hole in the wall in
close proximity to our fire. Mr. Bonner, who was
standing near, began to shovel them into the fire, and
continued to do so until he had put it out, without
however visibly decreasing the supply. Most fortunately, as far as man is concerned, the termites have
no lack of enemies, who are constantly on the look
out to destroy them. I noticed one day that a
number of them had taken up their residence in one
of my boots, which they had already commenced to
devour. On tipping them out on the ground, some
black ants rushed to the spot and carried them off,
intending, I presume, to devour them at their leisure.
In order to avoid their many foes, the termites
scarcely ever travel even the shortest distances without constructing for themselves a covered way made
of mud. A very common sight in Hausaland and
throughout tropical Africa, is a forest tree with its
trunk completely covered over with a layer of mud
so that no part of the wood is visible. This mud has
been put there by the termites in order to protect

themselves from birds or other enemies whilst they were ascending the tree in search of dry or dead wood. According to Professor Drummond, the inhabitants of tropical Africa are probably indebted to the termites for all the earth or soil of the country, just as we in England are indebted to the common earthworm for the same. If this be true, the termite may well claim to be the most useful insect in Africa or indeed in the world. It is however none the less certainly one of the greatest pests to which the traveller is liable, as it is practically impossible to take sufficient precautions against its ravages. On examining a certain book one day, I noticed that these termites had eaten away one of its covers and the first eleven pages of the writing. I was fortunately in time to prevent the rest of the book disappearing in like manner. The termite is very insignificant in appearance, being smaller than any English ant, its power being entirely due to its numbers and its capability of acting in combination. The following description is taken from Hartwig's 'Tropical World.' "At the end of the dry season, as soon as the first rains have fallen, the male and female perfect termites, each about the size of two soldiers, or thirty labourers, and furnished with four long narrow wings folded on each other, emerge from their retreats in myriads. After a few hours their fragile wings fall off, and on the following morning

they are discovered covering the face of the earth
and waters, where their enemies, birds, reptiles, ants,
cause so sweeping a havoc that scarce one pair out of
many thousands escapes destruction.   If by chance
the labourers, who are always busy prolonging their
galleries, happen to meet with one of these fortunate
couples, they immediately, impelled by their instinct,
elect them sovereigns of a new community, and con-
veying them to a place of safety, begin to build them
a small chamber of clay, their palace and their prison,
for beyond its walls they never again emerge.   Soon
after the male dies, but, far from pining or wasting
over the loss of her consort, the female increases so
wonderfully in bulk, that she ultimately weighs as
much as thirty thousand labourers, and attains a
length of three inches with a proportional width.
This increase of size naturally requires a corresponding
enlargement of the cell which is constantly widened by
the indefatigable workers.   Having reached her full
size, the queen now begins to lay her eggs, and as their
extrusion goes on uninterruptedly night and day at
the rate of fifty or sixty in a minute for about two
years, their total number may probably amount to
more than fifty millions, a wonderful fecundity which
explains how a termite colony, originally few in
number, increases in a few years to a population
equalling or surpassing that of the British empire."
Fortunately no species of termite has yet become

acclimatised in England, though several are found in the United States, and one species at least in the south of France.

Of the genuine ants the most troublesome that we came across were the Driver, or foraging ants, called by the natives *kwarikwasa*. They emerge from the forest and march through the country in a long, compact column, like a well-drilled army. If a house obstructs their way, they do not turn aside, but march straight through it, devouring as they go everything edible, including spiders, cockroaches, lizards, etc. Every creature, including the very largest, is devoured by them indiscriminately, unless able to make good its escape by flight. On the only occasion on which we were actually attacked by them, we were obliged to consult our safety in the same way. Dr. Barth tells of a somewhat similar attack which, however, he attempted to withstand without retreating. He says, " I had to sustain one day a very desperate encounter with a numerous host of these voracious little creatures that were attacking my residence with a pertinacity which would have been extremely amusing if it had not too intimately affected my whole existence. In a thick uninterrupted line, about an inch broad, they one morning suddenly came marching over the wall of my court-yard, and entering the hall which formed my residence by day and night they made straight for my store-room, but unfortunately, my couch being in their way, they attacked my own person most fiercely, and soon obliged me to decamp. We then fell upon them, killing those that were straggling about and foraging, and burning the chief body of the army as it came marching along the path ; but fresh legions came up, and it took us at least two hours before we could fairly break the lines and put the remainder of the hostile army to flight." *

One of the chief enemies to which all ants are alike exposed are the lizards. These are extraordinarily numerous and seem especially to frequent human habitations, where they make themselves useful by devouring all the ants and flies which come in their way. They are so quick in their movements that they catch and eat the common English housefly. They have constant fights amongst themselves, as the result of which it is a very common sight to see a lizard minus its tail, or, at any rate, with that member seriously curtailed. They very often sleep at night, clinging to a perpendicular wall or even hanging on to a roof. The traveller is occasionally woke by one dropping from this position on to his face.

One of the best known of the lizards and one frequently met with in this country is the chameleon. Apart from the singular power which it possesses of

* 'Travels in Africa,' by Dr. Barth, vol. iii. p. 398.

changing the colour of its skin, it is chiefly remarkable for the extieme sluggishness of its disposition. Wood says of this in his Natural History, " When it moves along the branch upon which it is clinging, the reptile first raises one foot very slowly indeed, and will sometimes remain foot in air for a considerable time, as if it had gone to sleep in the interim. It then puts the foot as slowly forward, and takes a good grasp of the branch. Having satisfied itself that it is firmly secured, it leisurely unwinds its tail, which had been tightly twisted round the branch, shifts it a little forward, coils it round again and then rests for a while. With the same elaborate precaution each foot is successively lifted and advanced, so that the forward movements seem but little faster than the hour-hand of a watch."

From the destructive point of view, the only rival which the ants and termites possess in Hausaland is the locust. In some years the destruction wrought by the locust far exceeds anything which they are capable of effecting. The year before last the locusts caused a famine throughout a great part of the Hausa States, an event which occurs, according to the information we received, at more or less regular intervals of eight years. Why they should multiply to excess in particular years it is at present impossible to say. Mahomet, according to the statements of his followers, once read upon the wing of a

locust, " We are the army of God ; we lay ninety-nine
eggs, and if we laid a hundred we should devour the
whole earth and all that grows upon its surface." " O
Allah ! " exclaimed the terrified prophet ; " Thou who
listenest patiently to the prayers of thy servant, destroy their young, kill their chieftains, and stop their
mouths, to save the Moslems' food from their teeth ! "
The words were scarcely spoken, when the angel
Gabriel appeared, saying, " God grants thee part of
thy wishes." It is believed to-day that the best preser-
vative against the attacks of locusts is this prayer
written out and enclosed in a reed stuck in the
ground. On two occasions we witnessed the passage
of a cloud of locusts over our heads. The natives
immediately turned out and commenced to beat
down as many as possible with nets, intending to
fry them for eating. Locusts will usually continue
their flight as long as the sun is shining, but as soon
as it begins to set they alight. However luxurious
the vegetation of the spot on which they happen to
encamp may be, before morning it will be almost as
naked and barren as the Sahara.

The description given in Exodus of the plague of
locusts in Egypt, would apply without the alteration
of a single word to several such plagues in Central
Africa within recent time : " They covered the face
of the whole earth so that the land was darkened,
and they did eat every herb of the land, and all the

fruit of the trees . . . . and there remained not any green thing, either tree or herb of the field."

From a sportsman's point of view, the chief animals which the country contains worth shooting are elephants, lions, leopards and antelopes. Elephants are still to be found in considerable numbers in the south-east part of Hausaland between the river Binué and Lake Tchad, also in the mountainous districts about a hundred miles to the north-west of Zaria. The natives often succeed in killing them armed with no better weapon than a flint-lock trade gun, or even with bow and poisoned arrows. Lions are to be met with frequently in the first named district, that is between the Binué and Lake Tchad, and leopards are common both here and in several other districts. Antelopes of several different species are extremely common throughout the whole country, though we found it very hard to get near enough to them to get a satisfactory shot.

Vultures and hyænas here, as elsewhere in tropical Africa, act as general scavengers. Were it not for their efforts, it is difficult to know how people could continue to live, at any rate, in the towns. As it is now, if any animal such as a dog, a donkey, or a camel dies, or if any putrid matter is thrown out during the day-time, before night the vultures will have removed almost every trace except the actual bones. If the same happens during the night-time, before morning the hyænas will have performed a similar office and will besides have eaten any bones which the vultures had previously left. On one occasion I counted thirty-three vultures sitting on the wall of our court-yard in Kano patiently waiting in the hope of our providing something for them to eat.

One of the very few animals kept in a state of captivity by the natives, is the Civet, sometimes called the Civet cat. It is a native of Abyssinia and of northern Africa, and is not, as far as I know, found wild in any part of Hausaland, but is kept by the natives for the sake of the valuable perfume which is obtained from it, and for which it was in former time so well known in Europe.

CHAPTER XII.

THE HAUSA LANGUAGE.

THE study of the Hausa language is of interest from three different points of view : first, because it is probably the language most spoken on the continent of Africa ; secondly, because of its close connection with the Semitic languages and the possibility that it may prove to have had a definitely Semitic origin ; and lastly, because a careful study of the language ought to furnish some clue as to the past history of the people by whom it is spoken.

First, then, in regard to the extent to which the language is spoken. In addition to the wide area in which it forms the dominant or exclusive language, it acts as a sort of *lingua franca* over practically all Africa north of the Equator, and west of the valley of the Nile. Its only rivals from the point of view of numbers speaking the language are Swahili and Arabic, but though either of these might claim to be understood over an almost equal area, neither of them is spoken by anything like fifteen million people, the number, that is, who are believed to speak Hausa within Hausaland itself.

Passing on then to the question as to what exactly is the connection between Hausa and the Semitic languages—or what here comes to the same thing, between Hausa and Arabic—the materials as yet available are insufficient to allow of a certain or satisfactory answer. Before indeed the question can be answered with any degree of certainty, it must first be ascertained what relation Hausa bears to the other languages by which it is immediately surrounded; such, for example, as the Kanuri spoken in Bornu, Nupe spoken in Bida and the surrounding country, and, what in this connection is probably the most important of all, Berber spoken north of the great Sahara. None of these languages have as yet been at all satisfactorily studied, though one or two books have recently been published on the last.

At first sight it would certainly seem as though Hausa had very strong claims to be regarded as a definitely Semitic language. Quite a third of the words which it contains are obviously connected with Semitic roots. Many of the commonest words, representing ideas or things with which the Hausas must have been familiar from the very dawn of their history, are Semitic; and lastly, the pronouns, which are usually regarded as the oldest and most distinctive possessions of a language, are Semitic too, with but a single exception which has apparently been borrowed from the neighbouring Bornuese language. Considering the fact that the country has for a considerable time past been subject to Mohammedan rulers, it would only have been natural to find that Hausa had borrowed from Arabic a large number of religious terms and words suggestive of a higher civilisation than that which existed prior to the Mohammedan conquest. The connection, however, between Hausa and Arabic is far closer than can be at all satisfactorily explained on the supposition that the one has been modified by the other, subsequent to the spread of Mohammedanism in the country. On the other hand, the objections to its being regarded as a Semitic language are very great, if not indeed insuperable. Not only is it the case that two-thirds of the vocabulary bears no resemblance whatever to Arabic, but the distinctive characteristic of all Semitic languages, namely, the possession of triliteral roots, is apparently wanting altogether.

The literature at present existing on the subject of the Hausa language consists of a grammar, dictionary and translations from the New Testament, made by Dr. Schön, who was formerly in the employ of the Church Missionary Society at Sierra Leone. Considering the fact that he never had the opportunity of visiting any place in which the Hausa language was spoken, and that he was dependent upon two freed slaves, neither of whom could read or write, for nearly all his results, his work has been wonderfully

well done. In addition to the above, Dr. Barth, a
German traveller, who visited Hausaland forty-five
years ago, has published some notes on this and
several other neighbouring languages which are of
considerable value. Lastly, an officer in the French
army has published a short vocabulary of Hausa
words collected in Algiers. As, however, he was
apparently ignorant of Arabic and dependent upon an
interpreter for his collection, nearly half the words
in his vocabulary are not Hausa at all but Arabic.*

Dr. Barth, in addition to a knowledge of Hausa
acquired by three years' residence in the country,
was able to converse in the Bornuese language and
had also devoted some time to Berber and Songai,
the latter being the language of Timbuctoo. He
believed that the Bornuese language, which is a language quite independent of Hausa and apparently
of a totally different origin, had been influenced to
a large extent by Hausa, which must therefore have
been developed anterior to it. He further gives it
as his opinion that Berber and Hausa belong to
the same class of languages. This opinion was, I
presume, grounded on the similarity of structure
between the two, as a comparison of the Berber and
Hausa vocabularies reveals remarkably few words
common to both.

* 'Essai de dictionnaire de la langue Haoussa,' par M. le Roux.
Algiers, 1886.

Nearly all who have written on the subject of the modern languages of Africa, though differing widely as to the details of classification, have agreed that the greater part of those hitherto examined may be grouped under one of three divisions—Semitic, Hamitic, and Bantu. The first includes Arabic and Ethiopic ; the last, a large number of languages south of the Equator, the distinguishing characteristic of the group being the absence of gender inflexion and the use of prefixed pronominal particles. The second division, which was once regarded as a sort of sub-division of the Semitic group, though now generally recognised as distinct from it, includes Coptic, Berber, and, not improbably, Hausa. Renan, in his history of the Semitic languages,* speaking of the limits of this group, says :—

" We must assign the Egyptian language and civilisation to a distinct family which we may call, if we will, Hamitic. To this same group belong doubtless the non-Semitic dialects of Abyssinia and Nubia. Future research will show whether, as has been conjectured, the indigenous languages to the north of Africa, the Berber and the Tuarek, for example, which appear to represent the Libyan and ancient Numidian, ought to be assigned to the same family. One important peculiarity of Tuarek and

* ' Histoire des langues Sémitiques,' par Ernest Renan. Tom. i. 2, 89.

Berber, the use of the prefix *n* as a sign of the genitive, is found also in Coptic. It appears, at any rate, as the result of the latest explorations which have been made in Central Africa, that the Tuarek is simply Berber apart from Arabic influence, and that a distinct family of languages and peoples extends in Africa from the Egyptian oasis, and even from the Red Sea, to Senegal, and from the Mediterranean to the Niger."

It is interesting to notice, in connection with the above statement, that the prefix *n* as a sign of the genitive occurs regularly in Hausa. The third reason, as stated above, why the study of this language should prove of interest, is that by such a study we ought to be able to gain some idea as to the origin and early history of the Hausa race, just as from the study of the Indo-European languages we have learnt many details in regard to the original home of these peoples, which reach back to a time long anterior to the existence of any written record. The study of the Hausa names for animals and plants, carried on in the light of recent zoological and botanical research, ought to give us some clue to the original home of the people using these names. To take one example. Tobacco grows apparently wild in nearly all parts of Hausaland, and might naturally have been supposed to be indigenous. The fact, however, that the word for tobacco, "tabba," is common to several distinct languages in the Central Soudan, of which Hausa is one, suggests that the plant had itself a foreign origin. This agrees exactly with what botanists tell us, viz., that it is a native of America, and was imported thence in very early times to West Africa. In some instances, however, the evidence is by no means equally clear or satisfactory, and we shall probably have to wait till a far more careful study of the surrounding languages has been made than has been as yet done, before obtaining the light from this source which we have a right to anticipate. There are certain animals now common in Hausaland which have been introduced within historical time. We should naturally have expected then that these would be found to bear similar names to those which they bore in their former home, and that we should thus have obtained some clue as to where that home was. Camels, horses, oxen and sheep are all introduced animals ; the two former probably came across the desert by way of Bornu, the two latter possibly from the east by way of Darfur and Wadai. In none of these four cases have I been able to trace any resemblance between the Hausa names and those which they bear in Arabic, Berber, or Bornuese.

To pass on then to any suggestions as to the original source of the language which we may obtain from the history of the people speaking it. According

N

to the information which I collected in Kano, the present king is the sixtieth who has as yet reigned. Nine hundred and forty-three years ago a section of the Hausa people, who were at that time collected in the neighbourhood of Daura, a town about three days' journey north of Kano, formed a settlement here under the leadership of a man named Kano, son of Bawo. Prior to this time there had been villages inhabited by people belonging to a different race on the summits of the two hills which are included in the present city, the Dala and the Goron Duchi. Kano built a wall around the whole, and established himself as king of the city which has since borne his name. He was a heathen, and was followed by twenty-four other heathen kings. Then Mohammed Rumpa, a mussulman, became king. He was followed by six heathen successors, after which all the kings were mussulmans. In 1802 of our era, Suleiman, a Fulah, made himself king, since which time all the kings have been Fulahs. The present wall of Kano was built by a king named Alwurri, one hundred and thirteen years ago.

According to the information collected by Dr. Barth, Kano was the son of Biram, his other children being Katsena, Zegzeg, Rano, Gober, and Daura. Their mother, according to the same tradition, belonged to the Diggera tribe. This latter fact is of importance, as the Diggera are a Tuarek tribe, and would thus suggest a connection between the Berbers and Hausas in very early time. Another interesting point in connection with this tradition is that Kano is said to have been appointed by his father as *sarikin baba, i.e.,* as chief of the indigo dyeing, thus showing that the dyeing of cloth, which forms so important a feature of the industry of Kano to-day, has existed for a very long time past.

Herodotus states that ten days' journey to the south-west of the Garamantes, who lived apparently somewhere north of the salt mines of Bilma, were a people called the Atarantes. This, however, he says, is not their national name, but designates them altogether. Barth suggests that this word Atarantes, or Ataras, as the singular form would be, is the Hausa *atara,* a word which means collected together. The identification is certainly somewhat precarious, but were it true, would tend to show that the Hausas, two thousand three hundred years ago, were living but a very short distance from the country which they now occupy.

On my inquiring from the most learned man I could find in Kano, as to what traditions the Hausas possessed in regard to their original home, he replied that, in very early time, prior to their settlement at Daura, they had come from the very far east away beyond Mecca. It is hard to say what importance is to be attached to this tradition, the existence of which is specially significant in view of the possibility of the language having been Semitic in its origin. My own opinion, however, in so far as I have been able to form one at all, is that Hausa is rather to be connected with the above-mentioned Hamitic, than with the Semitic languages.   It has been suggested that this at present ill-defined group represents an earlier stream of immigration into Africa than the Semitic, and that the resemblance between the grammatical structure of the two, points to that pre-historic time when both races or groups of races inhabited a common Asiatic home.   Should this theory ever be established, the interest, from the philologist's point of view, attaching to the study of what may perhaps prove to be the most important representative of the Hamitic group can scarcely be over-estimated.

Hausa has been reduced to writing for at least a century, and possibly very much longer.   The illustration here given of a sheet of a Hausa MS. affords a fair example of their writing.   This MS. is of peculiar interest, as it is the composition of Sheik Othman, who in 1803 preached a religious war, and, chiefly by the help of the Hausas themselves, succeeded in conquering the whole of Hausaland, and in establishing Mohammedan rulers in all the principal cities.   This song was circulated by him at the time, in order to induce people to take part in the proposed war.

In order to give the reader some idea of the sound

SPECIMEN OF HAUSA MS. [IT READS FROM RIGHT TO LEFT].

of the language, I append a transliteration of lines
two to six (line one being Arabic not Hausa) :—

   * Mu godi ubangiji sarakin sarota da ya aiko muhamadu
dan amina,

Muna zuba essalati bisa fiyaihi da umatan muhamadu ya fi
kowa

   Ku sorara jama elkaderawa halinmu da ankazana sai mu tuba,

   Da ya shi maibutulshi ba shi tsira, mu tuba mu beri butulshi
ko mu tsira

   Ku ber su maida eddini naasna abin ga da yinfa ya yi
ankakosai.

The vowels in the above are to be pronounced as in
Italian, the consonants as in English. The language
has a much softer sound than Arabic, lacking its
characteristic harsh gutturals.

It will be noticed that every word ends in a vowel
sound.

The language is peculiarly rich in forms of salutation. Two Hausas seldom meet each other on the
road without saluting, and, supposing them to be
acquaintances, they will sometimes continue repeating

   * The following is a translation of the above :—

We thank thee, O Lord, ruler of the kingdom, who hast sent
Mohammed, son of Amina.

We pour forth salutations on account of his excellency, and
of the friends of Mohammed, who excels all.

Listen, O companions of Abdelkadr, our evil deeds shall be
reckoned up unless we repent.

He who is ungrateful shall not be saved. Let us repent ; let
us put away ingratitude in order that we may be saved.

Leave off imitating the worship of the heathen. See what
Yinfa (King of Gober) did, and he was driven away.

various forms of salutation for several minutes at a time. If a man wishes to be thought learned, he will usually begin with the Arabic form of salutation, *salam alaik,* "peace be upon you"; to which the person saluted is expected to reply, *alaikum salam,* "upon you too be peace." The commonest forms of genuine Hausa salutations are preceded by the word *sanu,* which corresponds to our hail or welcome. Thus they will say *sanu du rana,* "good morning"; *sanu da aike,* "may you be happy over your work"; *sanu da gajia,* literally, "greetings to your weariness," *i.e.,* greetings be to you tired as you are. If a man meets you when it is raining, he will say, *sanu da rua,* "welcome to you and to the rain." The word is sometimes attached to the personal pronouns thus, *sanuku,* "welcome to you," and still more frequently it is used alone. Not unfrequently a man will repeat the word *sanu* a dozen times over in order to emphasize the force of his welcome. If the genuine feelings of a people can be in any way gauged by the number of forms of salutation and welcome which they possess, the Hausas would probably have little difficulty in establishing a claim to be the most affectionate people in existence.

Despite the fact that the Hausa language is spoken over so large an area, the difference between its various dialects is very slight. In this respect it contrasts most favourably with Arabic, the dialects of which differ so much that natives from different parts of the Arabic-speaking world often find the greatest difficulty in holding a conversation with each other. In the town of Sokoto the language has been influenced to a large extent by the Fulah, which is spoken there as the court language, but even a native of Sokoto seldom experiences any real difficulty in making himself understood elsewhere.

CHAPTER XIII.

MOHAMMEDANISM IN THE CENTRAL SOUDAN.

ABOUT one-third of the Hausa-speaking people profess the Mohammedan faith. This includes nearly all the Fulahs resident in Hausaland ; the heathen Fulahs, of whom there are still a considerable number, being found mostly to the west of the Niger. Mohammedanism, as has been before stated, became the dominant religion of the country about the beginning of the present century, having been forced upon the Hausas by their Fulah conquerors. In the large towns, perhaps, half the population are nominally Mohammedans, whilst the rest can scarcely be said to have any definite form of religion at all. Prior to the Fulah conquest they were pagans, but these would appear to have destroyed all traces of the idols which they formerly possessed. Except in Sokoto, where the Fulahs are specially numerous, no mosques are as a rule to be found. In Kano there is one small and miserable-looking mosque, which is, I believe, very seldom used, there is also one attached to the king's residence in Zaria. Amongst the Hausas themselves

MOSQUE BUILT BY FULAHS AT SOKOTO.

To face page 184.

there seems to be an entire lack of the religious fanaticism which characterises the Eastern portion of the Soudan. Although a large number of the people can read, copies of the Koran are but seldom to be met with. Even my teacher, Abd-el-kadr, who was one of the most learned men in Kano, only possessed a few selections from the Koran. We found it impossible to obtain any satisfactory information as to the exact form of idolatry which prevailed prior to the Mohammedan conquest. The only Hausa-speaking people who still possess idols are the hill tribes whom the Fulahs have never succeeded in properly subjugating, such as those whom we passed on our way from Kaffi to Zaria. These are naturally very suspicious of strangers, and we found it most difficult to extract any interesting information from them. One of the chief obstacles to the general acceptance of Mohammedanism is the existence of the Ramadan fast. The obligation which this imposes to abstain from all food and drink between sunset and sunrise during a whole month in each year is peculiarly trying in so hot a climate as that of Hausaland, and the keeping of the fast is in reality evaded by large numbers of those who profess to be good Mohammedans. The institution of Ramadan seems to me to be productive of two distinct evils. In the first place, it manufactures an unlimited number of hypocrites who profess to keep the fast, and do not do so; and in the second place, the reaction which occurs every night tends to produce revelling and dissipation of the lowest and most degrading type. Salam, our Arab servant, told us that in Tunis, where his home was, scarcely any one actually observed the fast, though all professed to do so. He and the members of his family always had a meal at midday, the doors of the house being first carefully fastened. Although the Mohammedan eating-houses were shut during the day, those kept by Jews remained open, and in these, he said, Mohammedans might always be found.

Immediately after Ramadan is held, the chief feast in the year, called by the Hausas *sallan laiya*. It occurred just as we were leaving Kano, and was the cause of our being delayed there for an additional two days. On this occasion, the king, accompanied by some thousands of horsemen and others, goes outside the wall of the city in order to offer up his prayers in public. This is apparently the only occasion on which the people generally come together for any religious service.

Although Mohammedanism is making very slow, if any, progress in the Hausa States, it has recently made rapid progress amongst the Yorubas who inhabit a country to the west of Hausaland, which has for its capital Lagos. Its introducers are for the most part Fulahs, the same tribe, that is, to whom the Hausas were indebted for their conversion to Mohammedanism at the beginning of this century.

The religion of the Prophet has within recent years found a considerable number of apologists in England, who, whilst professing Christianity themselves, have maintained that for a large portion of the human race, Mohammedanism is not only as good, but a distinctly better form of religion than that which they themselves profess. Inasmuch as Hausaland and the districts which border on it have so frequently been laid under contribution to furnish illustrations of the benefits conferred by Mohammedanism upon a formerly heathen race, it is worth while stopping to consider the arguments which have been adduced on either side.

Mohammedanism, it is often said, has conferred two distinct benefits upon the negro races of the Central Soudan. It has introduced a civilisation far in excess of what previously existed, and it has restrained its converts from the excessive indulgence in strong drinks which have proved so great a curse to those who have not accepted this religion. To take the last point first. Sir Gilbert Carter, the Governor of Lagos, in a letter recently published in the *Times*, says :—*

"It does not appear to have occurred to Bishop Tugwell that the best remedy for the gin disease exists and is in active force in the heart of the country about which he writes. It lies in

---

* *Times*, June 6th, 1895.

the encouragement of the Mohammedan religion . . . . the Mohammedan is naturally sober—it is a part of his religion—and no one can fail to be struck with the difference this habit of sobriety makes in the man; there is a dignity and self-respect about the Mohammedan negro which is looked for in vain in his Christian brother. It cannot be denied that Christianity and drink usually go together . . . . why not, then, recognise and utilize it (Mohammedanism) as a legitimate means for the re-generation of the negro . . . . it has more successfully exorcised the demon of drink than any other human agency."

If the relation between gin and Mohammedanism were as above described, it would certainly afford some ground for complacency in view of the spread of Mohammedanism in the Central Soudan. But that such a statement is absurdly wide of the truth is shown by the testimony of practically every traveller irrespective of creed and nationality. M. Binger, a distinguished French traveller in these regions, arguing in favour of the Mohammedan religion, as that best suited to the negro, says of the Fulahs, the most zealous Mohammedans in this part of Africa : [*] " All are Mohammedans without exception, and all are drunken in the fullest acceptance of the word. Towards five o'clock in the evening it is no longer possible to have a serious conversation with them ; young people, adults, and old men are all drunk." Joseph Thomson writes of the same part of the country in a similar strain : [†] " Everywhere you

[*] Cf. *Nineteenth Century*, September 1895, p. 444, note.
[†] Cf. *Good Words*, 1886, p. 27.

[*To face page* 188.

FULAH IN NATIVE DRESS OF COMMONER KIND.

find the same state of matters, and in many districts the wealth and importance of the various villages are measured by the size of the pyramids of empty gin bottles which they possess." To quote but one more witness, Captain Lugard, speaking of Hausaland and the hinterland of Lagos from which he has just returned, says, " In that part of the continent there are teeming populations eager to purchase our cottons and our hardware. But there too the barrier of exclusion, due in this case to Mohammedanism, has to be broken down. Over vast areas of West Africa, it (Mohammedanism) has become so deteriorated by an admixture of pagan superstitions and by intemperance, that its influence for good has been largely discounted. The Mohammedan negro is inflated with a sense of his superiority, which has taught him a supreme contempt for human life outside the pale of his own creed. The pagan is to him as a beast of the field fit only for slaughter or slavery. His religion has not taught him to condemn deceit, treachery or cruelty. Having raised him somewhat above the chaos and the superstition of the pagan, it has left him with no higher aspirations, the victim of bigotry and exclusion, the scourge of non-Mohammedan humanity."

It is quite true that in the Hausa States proper, the gin trade does not at present exist, but its absence is due not to the preaching of Mohammedanism, but to the action of the Royal Niger Company, which on gaining control of the river, stopped an already existing trade. In considering, then, the benefits which Mohammedanism has conferred upon the Central Soudan, it is impossible to credit it with having restrained its converts from the use of intoxicating drinks, or with having exercised any appreciable influence in this direction.

The question then remains, to what extent is it true that Mohammedanism has introduced into the Central Soudan a civilisation far in excess of any previously existing? Mohammedanism first began to exercise a dominant influence in Hausaland at the beginning of the present century. Nearly nine hundred years before this, if native tradition may be relied upon, the indigo-dyeing industry, for which Kano is so famous to-day, was in existence. Assuming this to have been the case, it is only natural to suppose that the manufacture of cloth was also in existence at that early date, a date at which the very name of Mahomet was probably unknown throughout the greater part of the country. The Hausa histories now available are almost exclusively occupied with lists of kings and their wars, and contain very few indications as to the civilisation which existed in early time; but what little evidence exists would certainly tend to suggest a doubt as to the extent to which the Hausas are indebted to the Mohammedans for their present remarkable civilisation.

Moreover, if it be true, as it probably is to some extent, that Mohammedanism has helped forward the Hausas in the path of civilisation, the assistance rendered here, as in every other country subject to Mohammedan rule, is by no means an unmixed good. Mohammedan progress, is progress up an *impasse*, it enables its converts to advance a certain distance, only to check their further progress by an impassable wall of blind prejudice and ignorance. We cannot have a better proof of this statement than the progress, or rather want of progress, in Arabia, the home of Mohammedanism, during the last thousand years. Palgrave, who spent the greater part of his life amongst Mohammedans, and who was so far in sympathy with them that on more than one occasion he conducted service for them in their mosques, speaking of Arabia, says :—" When the Koran and Mecca shall have disappeared from Arabia, then, and then only, can we expect to see the Arab assume that place in the ranks of civilisation from which Mohammed and his book have, more than any other cause, long held him back."*

The connection between Mohammedanism and slavery is so well known, that it is needless to

* 'Journey through Central and Eastern Arabia,' by W. G. Palgrave, i., p. 175.

dwell upon it here. Nor is it any reply on behalf of Mohammedanism to say, that until comparatively recent time, Christian nations were the largest slave-dealers of all in West Africa: for in the latter case the slave-dealing was carried on in spite of a professed Christianity; in the former, it is not only sanctioned, but actually enjoined by the religion of the Prophet.

Apart from the question of slavery, there is much to be said for the teaching of Mohammedanism, when regarded from a theoretical point of view alone. There are, for instance, many moral and religious sentiments contained in the Hausa poems, which I brought back with me, to which no Christian could take exception. But unfortunately Mohammedanism in theory and Mohammedanism in practice are two totally different things, and nowhere more so than in the Central Soudan. Nothing is easier than to draw an attractive picture of the benefits Mohammedanism might confer upon its converts, and of the high morality which its teaching might produce, and to bring extracts from the Koran and other Moham-medan sources which inculcate such teaching; nothing is more impossible than to find any country or people of which such a picture would be anything but a caricature.

Up to the present no serious attempt has been made on the part of Christian missionaries to settle in any part of Hausaland. The only point at which the Hausas have as yet come into contact with Christianity is on the river Niger, and more particularly at Lokoja. For upwards of thirty years the Church Missionary Society have had stations at various points on the banks of the Niger, but the results to be seen to-day bear but little proportion to the money expended and the length of time which has elapsed since the work was first commenced. The reason for this comparative failure has been that the C. M. S. have relied far too much upon native workers. The work was commenced soon after the disastrous attempt to explore the Niger by sending up Government gunboats in 1841. The

CHRISTIAN HAUSA-SPEAKING
NATIVE AT LOKOJA.

C. M. S., who were desirous of starting mission work on the river, recognising the extremely unhealthy nature of the climate, determined to work the mission by means of Christian natives introduced from Sierra Leone, with a native bishop as superintendent. This

o

plan, which sounds at once so plausible and so fully
in accord with the methods by which Christianity was
first propagated, has nevertheless been shown by
experience to be here entirely impracticable. In the
first place, it has proved impossible to obtain even a
moderate supply of natives as teachers or missionaries; and, in the second place, it has proved still
more impossible to find a suitable native to act as
bishop. The late Bishop Crowther was as remarkable and worthy a man as it would be possible to
find anywhere. Combined, however, with the most
transparent sincerity and earnestness, was a fault or
weakness which is universal with the West African
native, namely, want of power to control those over
whom he is placed.

Those who take an interest in the advancement of
the African native are too often tempted to forget
what history and evolution alike teach, that in regard
to the development of human character we must be
content to mark progress not by months or years but
rather by generations. It will certainly be several
generations before the West African native, however
carefully trained he may be, will have gained that
force of character which the Englishman now inherits
as a sort of birthright, and which will fit him to
be placed in an independent position of authority
whether in the service of the Church or the State.
Meanwhile the extraordinary progress which Chris-

tianity has made in Uganda, where a whole race has become at least nominally Christian, may well serve as an encouragement to those who desire to plant a Christian mission under careful European supervision, amongst this people whose acceptance of Christianity would bring us within measurable distance of the Christianising of all Tropical Africa.

CHAPTER XIV.

THE PILGRIMAGE TO MECCA.

MECCA is distant, as the bird flies, from the greater part of Hausaland, two thousand five hundred miles. By the route or routes usually followed by pilgrims, this distance is not infrequently doubled. There are, moreover, few if any portions of the globe where travelling is so slow, and is attended with so many dangers and difficulties. But these facts notwithstanding, the number of Hausa-speaking pilgrims to be found at any given time on their way to and from Mecca are to be reckoned by tens if not by hundreds of thousands.

When one realises the extremely slight influence which Mohammedanism exerts upon the great mass of the people, it seems strange that the numbers who annually attempt the pilgrimage should be so large. The explanation is to be found partly in the fact that the Hausas are naturally an enterprising people, and that a journey to Mecca affords them a convenient means of gratifying their love of adventure ; and partly in the fact that the journey, despite its risks and hardships, is from a money point of view by no means always unremunerative. Sir G. Goldie, speaking on behalf of the Hausa Association in the London Chambers of Commerce, said that on one occasion when travelling from Khartoum to Suakim he had fallen in with a caravan consisting of six hundred Hausa pilgrims, who were on their way to Mecca, but were at the same time acting as traders in the different countries through which they passed. This constant intercourse with Mecca has brought the Hausa people into touch, not only with it, but with countries such as Egypt and Tripoli, and has probably contributed to the attainment of the very remarkable degree of civilisation which exists to-day amongst them. An Englishman whom I met at Jericho and who had been down at Berber on the Nile, told me that he had there come across a Hausa native whose occupation was somewhat similar to one of Cook's tourist agents. He was in the habit of acting as conductor to parties of pilgrims to and from Mecca. Sometimes, as he explained, he brought them across the Sahara desert and thence *viâ* Tripoli and Egypt to Jeddah, the port of Mecca, sometimes through the very heart of Africa *viâ* Bornu, Wadai, Darfur, Khartoum and Suakim. This latter route has been to a large extent closed, owing to the action of the Mahdi, in recent years. A Hausa pilgrim in Tunis told me that he had travelled from Sokoto to Mecca by way of the Great Sahara ; but that his experiences in the desert, where he was at one time for ten days without water, had so frightened him that he was very reluctant to attempt the return journey by the same route. He accordingly started by sea from Tunis, going first to Malta and thence to Gibraltar, whence he hoped to get a French steamer to Dahomey, from which place he proposed to walk to Sokoto, a distance of seven or eight hundred miles. I met him again about six months later, when he told me that having got as far as Gibraltar, his resources had come to an end, and he had been therefore compelled to return, and was now contemplating trying the desert once more.

Whilst in Tunis he supported himself by selling charms, and it was his inability to sell these at Gibraltar that forced him to abandon his proposed journey. Every *haji*, i.e., pilgrim, on his return from Mecca, is believed to have acquired the power of writing charms capable of causing or curing disease, and of benefiting or injuring any given person. This, as can easily be imagined, is a most lucrative power to possess, and forms a sort of life annuity to the haji on his return to his own country. Hundreds of men, in fact, pretend that they have been on the pilgrimage, simply in order to establish their claim as writers of charms. An additional degree of sanctity, and therefore of power in regard to charm-writing, is supposed to attach to a man who has made the pilgrimage more than once. So far, however, is it from being the case that hajis are better men in the sense of being more truthful or trustworthy than others, that the exact opposite is usually true. If in buying or selling, one is brought into contact with a haji who has been on the pilgrimage once, it is safe to assume that he will make an attempt to cheat, if opportunity of any kind should arise ; if again one has to do business with a haji who has been on the pilgrimage twice, one may feel quite sure, he will be greatly dissatisfied should no opportunity for cheating present itself ; whilst if the haji in question be a man who has returned from his third pilgrimage, the stranger with whom he attempts to do business may take it for granted that, if no good opportunity for cheating should arise, he will refuse to do business at all. There is one spot in Mecca, which, one can only charitably presume, is but seldom visited by pilgrims from Hausaland. It is the enclosure which contains the Kaaba or sacred building considered the most sacred spot in Mecca. All who enter are pledged by the act of doing so, never again to tell a lie ! According to Burton, a large proportion of the pilgrims who visit Mecca refuse to enter this enclosure owing to their unwillingness to give any such pledge. Speaking of an Indian pilgrimage with which a similar pledge was connected he

says : " Amongst the Hindus I have met with men
who have proceeded upon a pilgrimage to Dwarka,
and yet who would not receive the brand of the god,
because lying would then be forbidden to them. A
confidential servant of a friend in Bombay, naïvely
declared that he had not been marked, as the act
would have ruined him.   There is sad truth in what
he said, 'Lying to the Oriental is meat and drink and
the roof that shelters him.' "*

The following brief sketch of the various ceremonies which the pilgrim has to perform on his
arrival in Mecca, is taken partly from reports received
from Hausa pilgrims and partly from the accounts
of Burckhardt and Burton both of whom actually
performed the pilgrimage.

The pilgrimage begins by a visit to Mount Arafat
outside Mecca, where a sermon is preached by the
Kadi to an audience which, according to Burckhardt,
sometimes numbers as much as seventy thousand.
During the course of its delivery, the Kadi is seen to
rub his eyes repeatedly, as the law enjoins the
preacher to be moved with feeling and compunction.
On the following day, the tenth of the Mohammedan
month Zul, the pilgrims proceed to a valley called Wady
Muna, where they perform the ceremony of throwing
stones at the devil.   It is said that when Abraham
was returning from the pilgrimage to Mecca, the

* 'Pilgrimage to Mecca,' by Sir R. Burton, ii., p. 210.

devil obstructed his passage at the entrance to this valley. On the advice of the angel Gabriel, Abraham proceeded to pelt the devil with stones, and having done this seven times the evil spirit disappeared. When Abraham reached the middle of the valley, the devil reappeared and appeared yet again at its extremity. On each occasion he was repulsed by Abraham in the same way. Small pillars six or seven feet in height are erected at these three points, and every pilgrim is expected to throw seven small stones about the size of a cherry at each of these pillars on three consecutive days. At the close of the first of these three days the pilgrims begin to kill the sheep or goats which they have brought with them for sacrifice. One Khalif in former time is said to have sacrificed on this occasion forty thousand camels and cows, and fifty thousand sheep. As soon as the sacrifices are complete, the pilgrims repair to the booths of the barbers to have their heads shaven, and the obligatory part of the pilgrimage being now ended, they put off their pilgrim dress and resume their former clothes.

To the north of Wady Muna is a hill called Jebel Thebeyr, which is visited by many pilgrims as being the spot where Abraham is said by them to have attempted to offer Ishmael as a sacrifice. The three days at Muna are spent in almost continuous feasting, after which a return is made by all to Mecca.

The remaining ceremonies which the pilgrim may perform, if he chooses, are drinking the water of Zemzem and entering the Kaaba. Zemzem is believed to be the well discovered by Hagar, when she was on the point of perishing with thirst together with her son Ishmael. The water, which is somewhat heavy to the taste, and of a milky colour, is believed to be an infallible cure for all diseases, provided the patient is only prepared to imbibe a sufficient quantity. Burckhardt tells of one of his fellow pilgrims who, when ill of fever, repaired to the well and drank so largely of its water, that he became almost unconscious; after which he lay on his back for several hours, till he had recovered sufficiently to start drinking again. When by this means he had brought himself to the very verge of death, he declared himself fully convinced that the increase of his illness was entirely due to his inability to swallow a sufficient quantity of this water.

The Kaaba, which, as has been already explained, is only entered by a limited number of the pilgrims, was, if Mohammedan tradition be true, constructed in heaven two thousand years before the creation of the world. Adam erected the Kaaba upon earth on its present site, which is directly below that which it formerly occupied in heaven. Ten thousand angels were appointed to guard the building from accidents, who, however, as its history seems to suggest, have been sadly remiss in the performance of this duty. Prior to the time of Mohammed, the Kaaba was adorned with three hundred and sixty idols. These he destroyed, and the place having been consecrated by him afresh, has remained ever since the most sacred spot which the Mohammedan world contains. The famous black stone, which is built into the wall outside, and is kissed by every devout Mohammedan, was given to Abraham by the angel Gabriel. It is said that its colour was originally white, and that it has become black in consequence of the sins of the pilgrims who have kissed it. It certainly requires but little credulity to believe that this portion of the tradition is true.

A large number of pilgrims, before commencing their homeward journey, pay a visit to Medina, which is about twelve days' journey to the north of Mecca, in order to worship at the tomb of the Prophet. This, however, is not regarded as an essential part of the pilgrimage, but is looked upon simply as a highly meritorious action, whereby many sins may be expiated. It is regarded in much the same light as a visit to the mosque at Jerusalem, or the Tomb of Abraham at Hebron.

On leaving Mecca the pilgrim carries with him the title of haji, which procures for him respect and assistance wherever he goes. There are some parts of the Soudan where it would be extremely dangerous for an ordinary Mohammedan stranger to travel, but where a haji could go with almost perfect safety. In the East the title is very generally accorded to the pilgrim who has merely visited the mosque of Omar in Jerusalem, but in Hausaland this pilgrimage is thought nothing of, and my suggestion to a Hausa Mallam that I too was entitled to rank as a haji, in virtue of my having visited this mosque, was not received with the respect which it deserved.

CHAPTER XV.

NATIVE CUSTOMS, ETC., PREPARATION FOR LEAVING
KANO.

BEFORE proceeding to give an account of our departure from Kano, I should like to add a few further
notes on some of the native customs which we
noticed either here or elsewhere in the Hausa
States.

Legacy duty in Kano is sufficiently high to satisfy
the most enthusiastic radical. Whenever a death
occurs, the property of the deceased is divided into
two halves. The chancellor of the king's exchequer,
or Maji, as he is here called, first of all arranges the
division of the property, and then selects the half
which he thinks would be of most value to the king.
Perhaps the chief disadvantage which this system
possesses, is that it affords too strong an inducement
to any sovereign, whose exchequer has become
depleted, to use measures whereby to unduly hasten
the decease of his more wealthy subjects.

Women occupy a much more favoured position
in Hausaland than in an ordinary Mohammedan

country. With the exception of the wives of the
king and one or two of his chief ministers, they are
not kept in seclusion, but are allowed to go about as
they please. With but few exceptions they have
freedom of choice in regard to marriage, and after
marriage the wife continues to retain her own personal property. In the event of her possessing any
slaves prior to her marriage, she retains these as her
personal servants, and should she leave her husband
would take them with her.

Gambling is even more common in Hausaland than
it is in England, and this, despite the fact that the
Hausas have no coins or metal currency. The most
common form of gambling is a game called by the
natives *chacha*. It consists in throwing up five cowrie
shells, the player winning or losing, according as the
shells fall, the right or the wrong way up. The game
is sometimes played with ground-nuts instead of
cowries. The Hausas become so excited over this
game that it is not an unknown thing for a man to
stake his own liberty and run the risk of becoming a
slave for life.

The administration of justice in the smaller towns
and villages is conducted by the king in person. In
larger places such as Kano, Zaria, etc., a judge called
the *alkali* is appointed to hear the majority of cases,
the more important ones only being reserved for
the king. An appeal is always supposed to lie

from the decision of the *alkali* to that of the
king, though the judgments of the former are seldom
reversed. If a stranger in the town become involved
in a lawsuit, the owner of the house in which he is
staying is supposed to appear and act as his representative or attorney. As no town, with the exception
of Sokoto, possesses any prison, the punishments
administered are necessarily of a summary character.
The most common are, mutilation, slavery and death.
In some towns, if a man is convicted of stealing, his
hands or feet are both cut off. The sentence of death
is usually carried out by beheading or cutting the
throat with a sword. If a man is unable to pay a
debt which he has incurred, his creditor may claim
him as his slave. Slaves who have committed any
crime or tried to run away are sometimes loaded with
chains and exposed in the market place or by one of
the gates of the city. There is, as might naturally
be supposed, a great deal of bribery practised, and it
but seldom happens that a rich man is condemned
unless it be for a distinctly political offence.

Burials in Hausaland take place either in the courtyard of the house in which a man dies, or outside the
walls of the town. There are no regular burying
places, no coffins are used and the grave is only made
about eighteen inches or two feet deep. A few
months after an interment takes place, no traces of it
are to be seen. In very few cases do the Hausas

trouble to construct a tomb in the orthodox Mohammedan style, that is with sufficient free space inside to
allow of the dead man sitting up.   It is believed by
the strict Mohammedans that three days after death
the corpse is visited by two angels, it then assumes a
sitting posture, and an examination is held into the
deeds committed during its lifetime and into its belief
in the Prophet.   Should the result of the examination
prove satisfactory, the soul of the dead man is carried
up to heaven by one of the two angels, if otherwise the corpse is severely beaten and punished by
the other angel.

Lucky days and the reverse are much regarded
especially when a man is about to commence a long
journey.   A man in Kano who took some of our
letters down for us to Lokoja, waited for a whole
week before he would start in consequence of a
declaration by a Mallam whom he had consulted on
the subject that no lucky day would occur before that
time.   It is supposed that if a man start on an
unlucky day, his whole journey will be unlucky, and
that he will be peculiarly liable to be robbed or
murdered on the way.   The discernment of these
days forms a scource of considerable profit to the
mallams who are fortunate enough to be accredited
with the possession of this power.

Many of the *names* borne by Hausas are suggested
by some physical characteristic, or by a resemblance

to some animal. The following are some of those most
commonly met with : Giwa (elephant), Baba (big, the
name of the present king of Kano), Bako (stranger),
Babankai (big head), Bawa (slave), Dauda, Gumbo,
Iderisa. The commonest of all is Mohammed, with its
two abbreviated forms Omadu and Momo. Several
Arabic names are very commonly used such as Ali,
Umoru, Othman, Abubekr and Abdelkadr.

To resume then the account of our stay in Kano
contained in Chapter VII., the following are a few
further extracts from the diary :—

February 10.—Dr. T. and Bonner seriously ill
with dysentery and Salam with black-water fever.
It seems probable that the cause of the dysentery
has been eating butter that had been washed in
native water. We shall take the precaution for the
future of boiling all butter before using it.

February 11.—Ellassar, our Hausa servant, informed me this morning that he intended deserting us
to-morrow. I told him that if he was going to commit
the crime of deserting us in the hour of our greatest
need he had better not wait till to-morrow, but go
to-day. I assured him at the same time that the
curse of God would overtake him wherever he went.
He however packed up his things and prepared to start
immediately. I then told him that I would retain his
property, and hand it over to the Maji, telling him

at the same time what he had done. After some further altercation I succeeded at length in getting him out of the house, and sat down to reflect on the ridiculously awkward position in which we were now placed. It was impossible for me to leave the house in order to look for another servant, and until I could find one I could get no food or firewood brought from the market. After half an hour or so, Ellassar reappeared to say that he had been to the Maji who had said that I must restore him his goods, and at the same time pay him ten thousand cowries which I owed him. As I knew that he could not have seen the Maji at this time of the day, I told him, in the most forcible Hausa I could, that he was, to use a Church Congress expression, a 'stranger to the truth,' and proceeded to eject him forcibly from the house. He then apparently altered his mind, and said that he had been thinking that it would not after all be right of him to desert us, and that he would wish to stay. Accordingly I agreed to take him back on the understanding that he should make no further attempts to go until we left Kano.

February 12. — Finished to-day the revision of the Hausa-English dictionary. I have verified or ejected every word in Schön's dictionary and have added nearly three thousand fresh words.

February 14.—The Maji sent yesterday three hundred thousand cowries ; we have now nearly half a million of money in hand. The musical box which we presented to the king on our arrival here, came back to-day broken, with a request that we would mend it. This however we were unable to do. It is hard to say whether vultures are guided to their food by their sight or their smell. I put two bones down on the ground close to our huts at a time when not a single vulture was in sight, but in less than three minutes I counted eighteen devoting their attention to them. The invalids are all a little better to-day.

February 19.—The king went out to war to-day to endeavour to drive away from his territory, Tukr the late king of Kano, who has just been expelled from Katsena. It would be hard to imagine a more unwarlike set of men than his warriors are. Dressed in every colour of the rainbow, they are apparently subject to no discipline of any kind. I followed in the wake of the army for some distance, about three hours afterwards, amidst a miscellaneous crowd of men, women, horses and donkeys. Judging by the rate at which they were going and their general gait, each man seemed possessed with an inordinate desire not to deprive those who had preceded him of the honour of bearing the brunt of the fight. Numbers of them were to be seen in groups of two or three lolling under trees within about five hundred yards of the gates of Kano. The headman in the Maji's house showed Dr. T. a large tin of yellow petals which, he said, Madugu (a man who tried to attach himself to us as a sort of agent) had given him, telling him that it was English tobacco that we had given to him. The stuff was not tobacco at all. He had thus made it appear that he was giving a present of some considerable value. Madugu has the reputation of being the greater liar in Kano, he must have spent the greatest part of his life talking in order to have deserved such a reputation.

February 22.—Dr. T. visited to-day a compound which contained thirty huts all inhabited by lepers. There is one in Kano that is said to contain no less than four hundred lepers.

February 23.—In a house visited by Dr. T. to-day, there were thirty-three lepers. In the same house were twenty-nine children of lepers, half of whom were grown up, whose parents had previously lived in this house, but not one of these children had developed leprosy. One leper had apparently suffered from his disease for thirty-six years. Swearing is extremely common here ; no sentence seems complete without an oath. As one man said of his fellow countrymen at Zaria, " their lips are heavy with the name of God, but there is no fear of him in their hearts." The Maji sent to-day two hundred thousand more cowries ; he still owes us sixty-five thousand.

February 25.—Arranged to sell the smaller of our two tents to the Maji for the king. The price is to be paid in donkeys, which he said will come to-morrow.

February 26.—About 6 P.M. a great disturbance occurred in the town, guns being fired off in all directions; on going out to see if war had suddenly broken out, we found that the feast of Ramadan had just begun. It begins as soon as the new moon becomes visible; according to my Greenwich Almanack the moon actually became new two days ago, but no one observed it here until this evening.

February 27.—A few days ago an Arab named Kulkul came to tell us that he was just about to send a messenger across the Great Sahara Desert to Tripoli and to offer to send any letters that we chose to entrust to his messenger. It appears that a rich Arab has just died in Kano, and it is thought desirable to communicate this fact at once to his friends in Tripoli. The messenger selected is a Tuarek, and the agreement is that he shall deliver the letters within forty-five days in Tripoli. He will travel on a running camel *viâ* Zinder and Asben. To get to Tripoli within the specified time he will have to travel nearly forty-five miles a day without a single break. I sent by this messenger who started to-day a packet of letters addressed to the English Consul at Tripoli, with a note asking him to forward them to England. [These letters reached England on July 1, the time occupied in transit being thus 93 days.]

I had quite expected to have been able to leave Kano by the beginning of March, but was prevented doing so, partly by the refusal of the Maji to pay the money due to us, and partly owing to a very serious relapse of dysentery, from which Dr. T. suffered, and which rendered it for some time impossible for him to travel. The Maji eventually informed us that his object in refusing to pay his debts, was to detain us in the town till the return of the king. A whole month was to elapse before we could make a start. Fortunately, as far as regarded the carrying out the objects of our expedition, this did not mean any actual loss of time, as the time was spent by me in collecting and translating some additional Hausa manuscripts and in other work upon the language. Besides obtaining original Hausa compositions, I secured several specimens of translation, from Arabic into Hausa. Having shown my teacher one day a copy of the New Testament in Arabic, he begged me to present it to him. In order to assure myself that he understood it, I asked him to translate a passage chosen at random into Hausa. This he did with scarcely a moment's hesitation, and apparently without a single mistake. I then told him that though I would not give him what he had asked for, I was willing to sell it if he was prepared to do some work in order to earn it. I told him to take it home and translate for me from Arabic into his own language the whole of the Gospel of St. John. In about ten days time he brought me this very neatly written out and, as far as I could judge, translated into good idiomatic Hausa. On his begging me then to give him the whole Bible in Arabic, I agreed to do so on the understanding that he would first translate in similar manner, the whole of St. Luke's Gospel. Later on, he translated for me the Sermon on the Mount, from St. Matthew's Gospel. I obtained also several translations from other Mallams, in order that I might be able to compare his work with theirs. These translations will form an exceedingly good basis for the publication of two at least of the Gospels in Hausa.

To resume the account given in the diary :—

March 14.—I gave my teacher to-day an advertisement of soap, written in twenty different languages, Arabic being the only one which he could read. Three days ago, I presented him with a copy of the " Greenwich Nautical Almanack " for last year, and told him that it was all about the moon and stars, and that by means of it we could predict the changes of the moon and the various movements of the stars. Since then, he has been endeavouring to learn the Arabic equivalents for the English letters, in the hope, I imagine, of setting up as an astrologer on the strength of this book. He does not, I think, know a solitary word in the English language. On

my telling him that Mars was probably inhabited, he
was greatly excited and wanted to know whether its
inhabitants were angels or men.

March 15.—One advantage of living in a tent, as
I have recently been doing, is that one is subjected
to visits from creatures which are sometimes more
interesting than welcome. I have learnt to accom-
modate myself to lizards, flies, beetles, mosquitoes,
white, black and brown ants, rats, mice, etc., but
last night a creature thought fit to make its peram-
bulations on the top of my head, which looked sus-
piciously like a centipede. After having demolished
it with no inconsiderable effort, another creature
resembling in appearance a diminutive octopus
paid me a visit. I received it, however, with such
extreme inhospitality, that it beat a rapid retreat,
and thereby saved its life, though its nervous system,
assuming it to have possessed such, must have
sustained a serious shock.

March 16.—As I was in the act of retiring last
night, Ellassar appeared with a look of terror on his
face, to inform me that a very large number of
thieves and brigands had broken into the town, and
were ransacking the place in the absence of the king
and his troops. We accordingly loaded our rifles
and prepared to receive them in a suitable way in
the event of their deciding to pay us a visit. After
waiting for their arrival for some considerable time,

we at length elicited from Ellassar the fact that by "very many thieves," he really meant eight. He none the less continued to assure us that we had good reason to be afraid, as they had medicine with them, by which they could render themselves almost invisible, and could come over the wall and creep along the ground without being seen. Such is the depth of stupidity to which Ellassar has sunk! With feelings better imagined than described, we retired and left him to look after the robbers himself for the rest of the night.

March 20.—I went to the market this afternoon to buy donkeys, in view of our setting out on our journey to the Niger. There were forty or fifty on sale, but they were for the most part a shocking set of skeletons covered over with broken pieces of skin. Having selected two, I proceeded to beat down the price from a hundred and twenty thousand cowries each to twenty-six thousand and thirty thousand respectively.

March 22.—The king came into the town this morning. It appears that he has killed Tukr. Tukr on leaving Katsena retreated to Kamri, one of the towns subject to Kano, the inhabitants of which were powerless to prevent his entry into their town. The result is that the king of Kano has burnt this town and carried off its inhabitants as slaves.

March 23.—To my great grief and distress a

member of our party died quite suddenly this
morning, after an illness of a few hours. This
morning early we found him lying down, and
supposing that he was simply idle, forced him to take
some exercise for the benefit of his health. About
twelve o'clock word was brought that he had
suddenly died, and that vultures had already commenced to eat him. The cause of his death is a
mystery, as he belonged to a family usually supposed
to be long-lived to a remarkable degree. The
member referred to was a jack-donkey, whom I
bought two days ago, and on whom I had been
depending to carry a hundred and eighty pounds of
our luggage. It really is a most tragic occurrence.

March 26.—Ellassar has gone home to see his
friends prior to accompanying us to the coast, before
going, he recommended us as a honest servant a man
called Baro. He has acted now as our servant for
twenty-four hours, during which time I have detected
him cheating or telling lies again and again. I
abused him vigorously, and told him what a bad look-
out, according to Mahomet, there was in the future
for liars, since which time he has bought one thing
for us without, I believe, attempting to cheat. There
seems to be no sense whatever of shame amongst
these Mohammedans. If you tell a man that he is
telling lies, as I have frequent occasion to do, he
simply laughs. Worse still, the people here seem to

assume, as a matter of course, that we are as great liars as themselves, and wonder that we should be so unwilling to own to the fact.

March 27.—As it would have been obviously impossible to get away without having paid a farewell visit to the king, I started at 6.30 this morning to see the Maji, in order to get him to take me to the king. On reaching his house, his attendants said that he had gone to the house of the king (this was a lie). I said that I should go there. On my way thither, they overtook me, and said that he had gone to the house of the Turaki (this was another lie). On reaching the king's house, I tried in vain to get an audience with his majesty. I was then told that the Maji had gone to the house of the Wazeer. On going there I was informed that I could not see the Maji as he was engaged. I at length succeeded in sending a message in to inform him that I was waiting outside, and received an answer to the effect that he would see me to-morrow. I returned an answer saying that I would not wait until to-morrow, and after considerable delay the Maji himself came out. He then told me that it was impossible to obtain an interview with the king to-day, but that he would obtain one for me to-morrow. In order to overcome his scruples I told him that if he would take me to the king immediately I would give him as a present the twenty-five thousand cowries which he had refused to pay us.

On reaching the palace, he told me to wait in the shade while he went in to see the king. Having waited an hour and ten minutes, my patience was completely exhausted. I accordingly got up and made my way, despite many remonstrances on the part of various attendants, to the audience room. Having sent a message in to the Maji to beg him to see me at once, he and the Turaki came out to inform me that the king was not willing to see us. I replied that we were just about to leave the town, and wished to bid the king farewell. They said that we could not leave the town for the present. I said that as I fully intended to leave immediately, it would be well to introduce me to the king at once. They returned to the king, and at length a message came out to say that I might come in. On doing so I found him sitting in a comparatively small room, the walls of which were all silvered over. As I entered a trial was going on of a man who was accused of having stolen a slave. The man was condemned, and was hustled off to be executed. I saluted the king and told him that we had found the air of his town was not good for us, and that we desired to leave. He said that we might go " gata," *i.e.*, on the third day. I replied that we desired to go " jibi," *i.e.*, on the day after to-morrow. After assuring him again that my companions were nearly dead owing to the bad air of his town, he gave his

[*To face page* 220.

HAUSA DRESS MADE OF DARK BLUE CLOTH, THE EMBROIDERED FRONT
FORMS A LARGE POCKET.

consent to our starting on the day I had named. I accordingly saluted him again and withdrew, my visit having taken me four and a half hours. I doubt whether the king ever had such a pressing visitor before.

March 28.—An Arab came this morning asking to see the Pasha, as he called me. He seems to have travelled a good deal, and to have known Gordon and Hicks Pasha, he showed me a fine sword given him by Major Grenfell in Egypt. I have now bought fourteen donkeys in addition to the one deceased. To-morrow being the great feast day of the year, it is doubtful whether we shall get off before the following day. Packing with the thermometer over 100°, and in the careful way absolutely necessary in view of our long journey, is most trying.

March 29.—Soon after midnight the Maji suddenly appeared. He came to say that the king had consented to our departure, and was sending us a present of an ox. This last was an exceedingly unwelcome piece of news, as it necessitated our sending a return present of at least equal value, and at the same time encumbered us with a creature of no possible use to us. On our explaining this to the Maji, he agreed to send us two donkeys in place of the ox. I went early this morning to take our return present, and after waiting about an hour, left the present at the Maji's house to be given by him to the king. About

2 P.M. we had finished packing up, and were ready to start, when Baro, our servant, came to inform us that the men whom we had engaged as donkey drivers had absconded, and that he himself was not willing to accompany us.

March 30.—Once again we have failed to get away, the men we had engaged having declined to start.

March 31.—Having secured, as we thought, a sufficient number of servants, we commenced to load the donkeys at 6 A.M. this morning. The operation was one of the most trying and disheartening in which I have ever engaged. Almost as fast as we put the loads on, the donkeys shook them off. After five hours of incessant toil we succeeded in effecting a start about 11 A.M. For a few yards all went well, then the loads commenced to come to grief one after the other. Our servants, four in number, were about as little use as if they had been made of stone. They never seemed to have seen a donkey loaded before, or to have the faintest idea as to how it ought to be done. With the greatest difficulty and exertion we at length reached the gate of the city, and camped for the night about a hundred yards beyond it.

CHAPTER XVI.

KANO TO BIRNIN-GWARI.

April 1.—All Fools' Day. There is an Oriental proverb which says, "Haste is of the devil, and tardiness from the All-Merciful." A belief in the truth of this proverb is one of the most desirable qualifications of which the European traveller in Hausaland can possibly be possessed. Yesterday I sent our servant, Baro, to the market to buy rope; soon after his departure our other servants absconded, and neither he nor they apparently intend to reappear. Happily a Bornuese man named Billama, whom we had not engaged, but who had followed us out of the town, has stuck to us. I rode into the market to-day, and made great efforts to engage some new servants, but without success.

April 2. — Detained here all day yesterday owing to our inability to find any more servants. Got up very early this morning and spent about two hours in loading the donkeys. Then occurred one of the common provocations of African travel. A man appeared, professing to have come from the Maji, to

say that one of our donkeys had been bought by us
from a man who had previously stolen it from its
proper owner, and that until the matter had been
investigated we could not proceed.   After some
discussion I arranged to go with the donkey in
question to the Maji, whilst the rest finished loading
the other donkeys and started.   Accordingly I rode
nearly two miles to the Maji's house, and finding him
out went on to the king's palace, where I succeeded
in finding him.   The matter in dispute between
myself and the would-be owner of our donkey was
investigated by the Maji, the trial, decision, and
sentence occupying in all about two and a half
minutes.   The decision was given in my favour.   It
was impossible for me to get to know the rights of
the case, but the fact that the man left the prosecu-
tion of his claim till we were in the very act of
starting suggests that his hope was that, rather than
allow ourselves to be delayed for the purpose of
investigating his claim, we would surrender the
donkey.   On returning to the gate I found that a
start had been made.   The trouble experienced in
loading was, however, so great, and so many loads
fell off *en route*, that I fear we shall have to return
to carriers once more as being the less of two evils.
After marching about seven miles we camped under
a tree just beyond the River Mallam.

   April 4. — Marched to-day about fifteen miles,

and after passing a place called Durung we camped on the far side of it, near to a small stream. For many miles after leaving Kano the country is almost level, with a few trees scattered here and there, but with practically no undergrowth. The firewood on sale in Kano market is nearly all brought from a distance of ten or twelve miles. Durung is a

GROUP OF NATIVES NEAR RIVER BINUÉ.

wretched-looking place with a tumble-down wall, and has apparently been recently raided for slaves. Between it and Kano there is a vast amount of land uncultivated, which, judging by the patches which have been planted, would well repay cultivation. Slave-raiding renders this at present impossible.

April 6.—Camped yesterday at Kabbo after a

march of seven miles. On commencing our preparations for departure this morning, we discovered that
two out of our five servants had absconded. Whilst
we were in the act of loading, a third followed their
example. The reason for their desertion is that they
are afraid to accompany us on the route we are
proposing to take, as it passes through some country
said to be inhabited by cannibals, of whom they are
horribly afraid. Having succeeded in engaging two
men to bear us company for the day, we marched
about fifteen miles, reaching a town called Karaii,
containing five or six thousand inhabitants. One of
our two remaining servants is a shocking cheat and
liar. He says that the reason why the other three
left us was that we gave the fifth man a tobe, and
did not give them one. He further suggests that if
we will give him one he will not desert. The powers
of sleep possessed by Salam our Arab servant are
astonishing. When shooting a bird yesterday I
fired from within two yards of his head, but he never
even stirred in his sleep. Our direction to day has
been S.W. ; yesterday it was W.S.W.

April 9.—The day before yesterday one of our two
remaining servants deserted us. He was such an
arrant scoundrel that we could not regret his going.
Just about this time a man appeared who had acted
as our headman on our march from Zaria to Kano.
He said that he had just finished his work and was

willing to be engaged by us. He agreed, moreover, to find two more servants. Having spent two days at Karaii, we came on this morning to Dunzo, distant about ten miles from the former.

April 16.—For the last six days we have been delayed here at Rogo, as I have been too unwell to march. The town contains a population of six or eight thousand. Most fortunately we had pitched our tents near to an encampment of Fulahs, from whom we were able to obtain a large supply of cow's milk, the first which I have had in Hausaland. On Friday last, which was Good Friday, we had the first rain since the twenty-fifth of October last. It came about 6 P.M. in the form of a violent tornado, which blew down one of our tents, and blew off the top cover of mine, but thanks to the energetic exertions of my companions it did not actually collapse.

April 17.—Got up very early in the hope of making an early start, but had to wait three hours in consequence of the non-appearance of our headman, who had stayed in the town last night. As neither Dr. T. nor I were quite up to the mark, we had arranged to go on a little ahead and wait for the rest further on. We had not gone, however, more than four hundred yards before we were informed that a party of horsemen from Katsena were approaching to make a raid upon the neighbourhood. Crowds of people could be seen shortly afterwards running towards the town in order to gain the protection which its walls would afford. As it was of course impossible to leave Bonner and our loads to be attacked, we returned to assist in the defence of our goods. The scare proved to be a false one, and after another hour's delay we all set off together.

April 20.—Soon after our arrival here (Denja), we did a most successful trade by selling pills. We bought with them from various patients, four fowls, a duck, four pigeons, five small heaps of rice, twenty eggs, five hundred cowries, and some guinea-corn for our two horses. One or two of the patients had followed us from our last halting-place.

April 21.—Missed the proper path to-day, and as a result went several miles out of our way. Ellassar, our old Kano servant, turned up to-day to our great satisfaction. He had been wandering in search of us for about a fortnight. The inhabitants here are very much afraid of a man called Ba-Gudu, who is camped not far off. He is a son of the Sultan of Sokoto, and goes about from place to place plundering and murdering indiscriminately. It is a little uncomfortable having him as such a close neighbour, especially as we are compelled to remain outside the city in order to get food for our donkeys. For several days past we have been travelling through country which has not apparently been visited before by any

European. We have accordingly been greatly troubled by the unlimited curiosity of the people, who crowd around us from morning till night. A further difficulty is that our map now affords us no information, and we are dependent upon native reports in selecting our route from day to day. We are now over a hundred miles from Kano. Bought a piece of wood from the kedania or shea-butter tree. It is red like cedar, and extremely hard, almost as much so as the iron-gum, which I remember in Australia.

April 25.—Detained here (Maska) for three days, Dr. T. being too unwell to travel. Dismissed our headman before starting this morning for incorrigible idleness and dishonesty. The country through which we are passing now is fairly well wooded and has a considerable undergrowth. In order to cross one stream to-day we had to take all the loads off the donkeys and carry them over separately. This caused a delay of an hour and a half. I got fairly lost in the forest to-day whilst endeavouring to shoot some guinea-fowl. It is a most uncomfortable thing suddenly to discover that one has completely lost the direction of the camp, when one has nothing but two or three shot cartridges for food or defence.

April 26.—Yesterday evening a most dire calamity befell us. The last of the three filters which we had

brought with us broke. Henceforward we shall have
to drink boiled mud. Camped to-day at the half-
deserted town of Idesu. There are said to be
elephants in our immediate neighbourhood, but we
have not been fortunate enough to come across
any.

April 27.—After going a few miles to-day, the
path became most indistinct and uncertain. As none
of our men had been this way before I attempted to
act as guide. As, however, the place to which we
were steering is marked in no map, and we did not
know its direction to within several points of the
compass, the duties of guide were somewhat arduous.
Soon after midday, having previously passed several
burnt and ruined hamlets, we passed a large deserted
town, and camped in the forest a little way beyond it
near a small stream. The existence of a considerable
number of pools of water at the end of the dry
season, throughout the country which we have been
recently traversing, tends to show that this country
could easily be inhabited and cultivated to a far
greater extent than is at present the case, if only the
perpetual civil war resulting from slave raiding could
be abolished. This part of the country is at present
very sparsely inhabited, as may be gathered from the
fact that during a march to-day of eleven or twelve
miles we did not pass a single person. Several of the
ruined hamlets which we passed had evidently been

very recently destroyed, as the crops had been left unreaped in the ground. A heavy rain and thunderstorm which occurred to-day cooled the air considerably, our thermometer falling to 88°.

April 28.—During our march to-day we passed a number of huge rocks weighing perhaps from three hundred to a thousand tons. They were scattered about our path for several miles. Their general appearance is not unlike that of the well-known Brimham rocks in Yorkshire. The stones are of stratified rock. We are camped to-night at the half-deserted town of Zogendowa. As we have failed to persuade its inhabitants to sell us any food, our men are in a distressed condition, and are eating the stringy fruit of the shea-butter tree. We have for ourselves a little rice and a few small yams. It appears that we are still two days' march from Birnin-Gwari, though at Maska four marches back we were told that we were within one day's march.

April 29.—Soon after starting this morning we came to an apparently insignificant track branching off south to Zogendowa, from the west gate of which we had been told there was a path leading to Birnin-Gwari. As our path continued west, which was the direction it had kept all day yesterday, and as paths in Africa seldom change their direction without some obvious reason, I continued along it. However, after going about a mile it began to turn W.N.W., N.W., and finally N.N.W. This was so obviously wrong that at length we abandoned it and struck south through the bush. This was most precarious travelling as at any moment we might come to a place which loaded donkeys could not cross. After wasting about an hour and a half, we eventually struck the true path, and continued along it all day marching altogether fourteen or fifteen miles.

April 30.—Got up at 3 A.M., in anticipation of reaching Birnin-Gwari. We crossed a large number of very deep gullies, very few of which, however, contained any water. We reached our destination soon after midday, after a march of about nineteen miles. Instead of finding a flourishing town, there was nothing to be seen but a mass of burnt and deserted ruins. It appears that the king in whose territory it lies had recently made war upon it, and after a long siege had captured it, and sold its inhabitants as slaves. This king, whose regular capital is the town of Kwontagora, bears the magnificent title of King of the Soudan. As it was obviously impossible for us to stop, we continued our march for another seven miles in order to reach Sansanni, the place at which this king was encamped. We arrived at 2.15 P.M. utterly wearied out with our long march of nearly twenty-six miles. The camp consists of a large collection of huts built entirely of straw, its general appearance being far from imposing. As we approached it, we came across a dead donkey, two dead horses, and a dead man lying by the side of the path. The latter had had his two feet cut off for some imaginary crime. He had evidently crawled along till he could do so no longer, and had soon after become a prey for the vultures. He lay there in mute appeal to Heaven against the wickedness and cruelty of his fellow-men. Having passed round the north corner of Sansanni, we camped about a mile outside the west gate, near some water, or rather some semi-liquid filth which our men called water. The situation of our camp is most dreary. There is no grass or food of any kind for horses, donkeys, or goats. The donkeys, moreover, are greatly overdone with their long march. Almost immediately on our arrival the king sent a message to express his surprise at our not having sent a messenger to greet him. I replied that I would come in person to do so on the following morning. During the evening a violent thunderstorm broke over us. As this put our fire out and stopped our cooking, we had to go tired and half-starved to bed. All food on sale in the place seems to be fabulously dear as compared with any other town which we have as yet visited. The king, so we are told, spends part of the year at his capital Kwontagora and part of it here. His object in coming here is to levy tribute on the caravans which pass this on their way to or from Bida and Kano or Zaria. Lying as it does on such an important trade route, the king is enabled to collect a considerable revenue from the native traders, and more especially from the kola-nut caravans, all of which must pass this way.

[To face page 234.

NUPÉ BEGGAR, ILLUSTRATING THE AMOUNT OF CLOTH OFTEN WORN.

CHAPTER XVII.

BIRNIN-GWARI TO BIDA.

THE king of the Soudan is an object of greater fear alike to his unhappy subjects and to the native traders who have occasion to pass through his territory than any other king in Hausaland. The country over which he rules is about two hundred by one hundred and fifty miles in extent, and lies to the south of Sokoto and to the north and north-east of Bida. For some days prior to our arrival at his camp we had been hearing of various atrocities of which he had been more recently guilty; and had it been possible for us to have avoided passing through his territory, we should undoubtedly have done so. The first intimation of coming trouble was the fact that he sent no present to greet us, but a message instead to express his displeasure at our not having sent on beforehand to greet him. On the day following our arrival I went myself to pay a visit to the king, taking with me a carefully selected present worth there about twelve pounds. He is a man of about thirty-five, and was reclining in a large straw-

built hut, surrounded by a number of his courtiers.
On my spreading out the present before him, he
expressed no immediate dissatisfaction, but said that
he would send us as a return present a goat and some
rice.   The latter never came; the value of the former
was scarcely a twentieth of the value of the present
which I had just given him.   On leaving him I hoped
that our present had really satisfied him, and that we
should have no further trouble.   In this, however, as
the sequel will show, I was sadly disappointed.

May 1.—On my return from my visit to the king,
I was followed by one of his brothers who did his
utmost to extract a present from us for himself.   I
gave him a Norwegian knife, which produced anything but satisfaction on his part.   Soon afterwards
the king's professional fool came howling and shrieking around us in order to obtain a present.   I sent
him out one cowrie, which is here equal to about the
one hundred and twentieth part of a penny.   This
was so much more than he deserved, considering the
noise he had made, that one could almost wish the
currency of this country still further sub-divided in
view of such emergencies.   Soon after midday the
brother of the king, to whom I had given a knife
reappeared.   He began by complaining that we had
given no present to the man who had brought the
goat sent by the king.   On our offering to do so, he
went on to complain, on behalf of the king, that I

alone had been to see him, and further stated, what was no doubt the real object of his visit, that the present which I had given to the king was much too small, and that I had insulted him by offering it. On my saying that I could not increase it, he said that we must pack up our goods and go into the camp of of the king, as he intended to detain us as prisoners. On his way up to our camp he had found our servant Ellassar engaged in buying food for us in the market. He had thereupon pitched over his cowries and driven him out of the market, telling him that he was on no account to buy us any more food. This greatly increases the awkwardness of our position, as we have only food in hand sufficient for a single meal, and have no means of obtaining any more. In reply to the demand of the king's brother that we should bring our goods into his camp, I said that whatever happened we should never consent to such a proposal. He then became exceedingly violent, and threatened to murder us all. I suggested that in the event of his doing so he would be the loser in the long run, as no other white man would ever come to his country. This, however, produced quite the opposite effect to that intended, as he at once replied that this was the very thing he desired, as he never wished to see any more white men. I then pointed out that, although we were very few in number, our rifles were repeating rifles, and that though he could no doubt eventually overpower us, it would not be before we had killed a considerable number of his own people. As we were still talking, a messenger from the king arrived bringing back our present which he had rejected. Matters began thus to look serious, and it was obvious that something must be done immediately to prevent an attack being made upon us by the king. As it was evident that this brother of the king had influenced him against us, the first thing to be done was to gain him over to our side. I accordingly told him that we would double the king's present, and would at the same time give him a large present if on his part he would guarantee that the king would allow us to leave the place. He thereupon asked to see what exactly his own present was to consist of. A very long time was consumed in bargaining in regard to his present, the final result being that we had to give him nearly ten pound's worth of goods, chiefly consisting of rolls of silk. He left the present for the time being, saying that as soon as it became dark he would return to take it away. His object in waiting was to prevent the king discovering that he had received a present. Before leaving he definitely promised that the king would not again return his present, and that we should be allowed to leave on the following morning. He, however, dropped some hints as to the possibility of the king sending after us and bringing us back as his prisoners. He had

scarcely gone before a messenger from the Dan-
Galladima, an official who professes to have greater
influence than any one else with the king, arrived
bringing us a present of five thousand cowries and
demanding a return present. This we were compelled
to give, as also a present to the man who brought
the message, and to the man who brought the
cowries. The king's brother on taking away his
present to-night promised repeatedly to send us some
rice, which has not, however, arrived. If we are not
prevented by physical force, we shall try to leave this
to-morrow, despite the fact that our donkeys are
quite unfit to travel, and that we have practically no
food in hand.

May 2.—Got up this morning about 3 A.M. quite
uncertain as to whether we should be permitted to
leave Sansanni or not. After starting we had to skirt
for a long distance the edge of the king's encampment,
and were more or less expecting every minute to see
some of the king's soldiers emerge to drive our
donkeys inside, than which nothing would have been
easier. However, we proceeded unmolested, and
marched in all about twenty-two miles. One of our
donkeys fell down on the way to rise no more, and
a second had to have its load carried by two men
and march without any. Our men are fortunately
thoroughly frightened, and are therefore willing to
march as fast as is in any way possible. We have no

yams or rice, our only food being a small bag of flour which we brought with us from Kano. By mixing this with hot water we make a sort of food and drink combined. We are camped a little short of a ruined place called Kiranku.

May 3.—We had to abandon another donkey to-day to the tender mercies of the vultures. The country through which we passed to-day was for the most part thickly wooded and constantly intersected by very deep gullies. Our food supply is most distressingly low. Our men have managed to find some roots in the ground which they are eating, but it is almost impossible for us to imitate their example. The worst of the situation is that we have now ascertained that his imperial majesty of the Soudan has ravaged the country for something like sixty miles in the direction in which we are marching, so that there is but a poor prospect of our getting anything to eat for two or three days more. Why he did not carry out his threats and seize all that we possessed is very hard to understand. My respect for his sagacity is largely diminished by his not having made better use of his opportunity. We are camped to-day by a small pool of water near to a half-ruined place called Bugaii, distant about sixteen miles from our last camp. The few inhabitants left in the place refuse to sell us any food. Soon after our arrival a message was brought to us to the effect that a son of the

Sultan of Sokoto was in Bugaii, that he had intended going to-day, but having heard of our coming, had stopped, in order that he might have the pleasure of accompanying us. It is very unlikely that one of the sons of the Sultan is here, though they are fairly innumerable, but this message is probably the first stage in an attempt to extort a present from us. Our donkeys have degenerated into a procession of invalids, but as we are half-starved, and as this message suggests the possibility of further interference with our movements, we must proceed unless actually prevented. 9 P.M.—Our food supply has suddenly improved ; Bonner has succeeded in shooting a guinea-fowl, and the inhabitants of this place have sold us some oil which has about the consistency and appearance of lard. We have on several previous occasions used it for burning in a lamp. By mixing it with flour we have been able to manufacture some pancakes, which are a great improvement in the way of diet on nothing at all. The reputed son of the Sultan of Sokoto turns out to be nothing more than an ordinary Sokoto merchant who had sought to impose upon our credulity by calling himself a son of the Sultan. During our march to-day we passed a man who had apparently given up the struggle for life in despair, lying across our path. The vultures had already commenced to eat him.

May 4.—After a march of about fifteen miles

R

to-day, we reached a large village called Wuri-Kenkina, where we obtained good water and grass, but no food. Dr. T., however, shot a large bird called by the natives *goraka*, which measured six feet from the tip of one wing to the tip of the other. Bonner shot three guinea-fowl, so that we were not at all badly off.

May 5.—Sunday. Resting here to-day. It is a great pleasure to get a quiet Sunday after having had so many lately of a different character.

May 6.—After a march of nine miles we reached a place called Dawakin-Basa, which is distant sixty-three miles from Sansanni, and lies just beyond the district recently raided by the king of the Soudan. Here, for the first time since leaving Sansanni, we were able to buy some food. It consisted of a diminutive quantity of exceedingly bad rice, largely mixed with stones.

May 7.—Camped to-day at a place called Nassarawa, the third of this name which we have come across. Some of the people here speak a language called Kamuku, which is quite different either to Hausa or Nupé. Its numerals, which I got by inquiry from them, from one to ten are, *iyo, dero, tatu, nashi, ta, tunhi, tunderu, tutatu, tundashi, ufa,* twenty is *ufaliu,* thirty, *ufatatu,* and hundred, *dari.* This last is the same as in Hausa, and has probably been borrowed from it. Water is *muni,* rain, *shiro,* God, *tundia.* The personal pronouns are *gemu, hanike, kanyam, gemu, mushes, amrasu.* This language is apparently spoken by a large number of the heathen people who live in the mountainous districts to the north-west of this.

May 9.—We passed to-day a caravan consisting of about four hundred carriers and a hundred and fifty donkeys, most of which were carrying salt. We started to-day in the expectation of reaching a place called Karamin Ungué after a march of about ten miles, but after we had gone about this distance, no such place appeared, nor any water, so that it was impossible for us to stop. We had to march in fact another ten miles before finding any, the last half of our journey being over very hilly and rocky ground, where it was often rather more than our donkeys could do to keep from falling. We passed several minute villages perched on the summits of steep hills which had, however, no visible water supply. The water near to which we at length encamped, consisted of four dirty puddles in the dry bed of a stream, some of which had just been used by the natives of Karamin Ungué for washing their dirty clothes in.

May 10.—Having packed our goods by moonlight, we succeeded in getting started at 5.45 A.M. We marched during the greater part of the day in the midst of, and mixed up with, a native caravan consisting of some hundreds of donkeys. After pitching our camp I went out to endeavour to shoot something to eat, and after wandering for several miles I made again the uncomfortable discovery that I had lost my way. However, after changing and rechanging my direction, I came at last quite unexpectedly upon our tent just as Dr. T. was in the act of despatching a man to search for me. We are said now to be only nine days' march from Bida ; this latter having been frequently visited by Europeans has a home-like sort of sound. According to our boiling-point thermometer, Ougou, the place near to which we are now encamped is 950 feet above sea-level. Reading Wordsworth's "Tintern Abbey." In a country such as this, one may well be excused loving, as it were, the spirit of nature more than that of humanity. The hopeless selfishness which seems to pervade every word and action of the inhabitants here is absent when one turns from man to nature, and its absence produces a feeling of wondrous joy and relief. Happy indeed is it that history records one life on which the mind can dwell, which produces no such discord as our own and the lives of those around.

May 13.—Another of our donkeys died during the night. The scenery through which we passed to-day was very fine, though, owing to the hilly nature of the ground, we were considerably delayed. Shot to-day a bird called by the natives *shafo*, about the size of a large pigeon. As neither Ellassar nor I had a knife, wherewith to cut its throat, as required

by the Mohammedan law, Ellassar cut or rather pretended to cut it with a piece of grass, the bird having
been already killed by the shot. There is a native
caravan detained here (Goumna) owing to their
refusal to pay more than three hundred thousand
cowries, *i.e.*, about twelve pounds. At Ougou, the
last place, they were compelled to pay four hundred
thousand, and at Sansanni the same amount plus
four goats.

May 14.—Had breakfast this morning at 2.30 A.M.
in the hope of getting started before a native
caravan, which was camped close to us. As we were
in the very act of starting it commenced to rain with
indescribable violence. Our tent having been already
packed up, we could obtain no satisfactory shelter of
any kind, and soon became almost as wet as it is
possible to be. It continued to pour without inter-
mission for five hours. At the end of an hour and a
half, we succeeded in erecting our tent, but though it
was supposed to be the best obtainable for money
in London, it completely failed to keep out the rain,
which came steadily dropping through the green
waterproof canvas. The few disconnected water-
holes in the dry bed of a stream close by became in
the space of two hours a rushing and impassable
torrent. When the rain at last abated, we felt
something like Noah at the conclusion of the flood.

May 16.—Tasted a fruit called, by the natives,

tuo. It grows on a climbing stem, and is about the size and colour of a large lemon. It has a very bitter taste, and is filled with hard stones about the size of plum stones. These our carriers swallowed, apparently with great relish. We reached to-day the river Koduna, which we crossed eight months ago at Gierko. Its bed is half a mile in width, though the actual stream is not now more than two hundred and fifty yards across. It has been steadily rising in consequence of the approach of the rainy season, and in a few days' time will probably cease to be fordable. The crossing, which occupied an hour and a half, was a most picturesque sight. The donkeys came across swimming with their heads and ears just above water, all the loads being taken off and carried on the heads of carriers. We are most fortunate in having arrived before the river became too deep to ford, as we are informed that the last white man who crossed here was delayed by the ferryman for no less than three days, and was eventually charged the exorbitant sum of one hundred thousand cowries for his passage over. At the point where we crossed, just opposite the town of Wushishi, the river is flowing from north-east to south-west. In the wet season loaded canoes go down from here to the Niger.

May 17.—Owing to a violent rain-storm, which occurred last night, the river, which we crossed

yesterday, is quite unfordable, and will probably
remain so for the next six months. One man is said
to have been drowned to-day in attempting to cross.
The king of this place is a Nupé, and so are the
majority of the inhabitants, although the place is
included in the dominions of the king of the Soudan.
This would seem to suggest that in earlier time the
Koduna formed the boundary between the territories
of the latter and those of the king of Bida. Dr. T.
and I had arranged to go in search of a hippopotamus
last night, which had for some time past been
residing in a neighbouring island, but we fortunately
discovered from the canoe-man, who was to take
us over, that the hippopotamus had changed his
residence, and so saved ourselves the trouble of a
useless search.

May 18.—A marked change in the character of
the scenery has taken place since we crossed the
Koduna. The country is now very nearly flat and
much more closely wooded. In many places the
creepers, which join the trees of the forest together,
make it impossible to diverge from the footpath in
any direction. Tree ferns, palms, and rich luxuriant
grass abound. At the place at which we are camped,
near to a small village called Karamin Ayaba, the
monkeys are running about and screaming over our
heads. One of our party wished to shoot one of
them, but I objected on the ground that the murder

of one's near relations can never be otherwise than wrong. I shot a bird for our supper called by the natives *chilikowa*, which is said to live upon locusts.

May 21.—We entered to-day the territory of the king of Bida. Judging by the number of unwalled villages and the general appearance of prosperity, the inhabitants would seem to be enjoying a far more secure life than the subjects of the king of the Soudan. A large proportion of the land around here is under cultivation. We are hoping to reach Bida the day after to-morrow.

May 22.—Reduced to shooting doves to-day in default of anything better to eat. They abound in almost all parts of Hausaland. In close proximity to our camp is a small village inhabited only by women, who, to judge from their appearance, must all have been selected on account of their ugliness. I never saw such haggard, dreadful-looking specimens anywhere. Several of the villages which we passed yesterday were inhabited by slaves belonging to the king of Bida, who were engaged in cultivating the adjacent fields for his benefit.

CHAPTER XVIII.

BIDA TO EGGA.

ON May 23, after a march of about fifteen miles, we pitched our camp outside the walls of Bida. A sudden attack which was made upon us here, owing to an unfortunate misunderstanding on the part of the natives, very nearly brought our expedition to an abrupt close. At the date of our arrival at Bida the latest political news which we had received from Europe was nearly six months old, and we were quite unaware of the fact that the French Government had sent two or more armed expeditions for the purpose of asserting a claim which she had recently put forward to the inclusion of Borgu within her sphere of influence. About the beginning of May one of these expeditions had crossed the Niger from Borgu and had destroyed a village situated within the territory of the king of Bida. The news of this had, of course, been carried to the capital, and had created a wide-spread feeling of hostility to Europeans in general. The people had, however, learnt to distin-guish between the French and the English as represented by the Royal Niger Company, with whom they had a formal treaty, and whose station at Egga was within seventy miles of Bida. Had we approached the town from this side we should probably have been received with all due hospitality. Unfortunately we were approaching from the opposite direction, and it was therefore not to be wondered at that the people failed to connect us with the white men who lived at Egga, but assumed that we could only be approaching Bida with some hostile intent. The account of the reception we met with is briefly as follows. On nearing one of the gates on the north side of the town, Dr. T. at my request rode on in advance to select a site on which to erect our tent. The spot fixed upon was beneath the shade of two large trees, a spot at which, as he was informed, a white man had once before encamped. As we approached, a man came up, obviously intent on picking a quarrel with us, and in a very excited way ordered us to keep our donkeys from approaching some guinea-corn which was growing near to the path. With this demand we immediately complied, and I doubt whether the donkeys got the opportunity of eating a single grain. On reaching the trees, one of our servants came to me and complained that this man had attacked him, showing at the same time large weals on his skin where he had been struck. Twenty minutes later the man himself came up, and I

asked him then why he had attacked my man. As
his reply was extremely insulting I said that when we
went to see the king I should report the matter to
him. Without any further parley he rushed up and
struck me a blow on the head. As I was extremely
anxious that the matter should proceed no further, I
did not return his blow, but, pointing to our rifles
which were leaning against one of the trees, I told
him that he should be careful how he attacked people
who were quite capable of defending themselves
should they have occasion to do so. I was sitting
at the time in a chair at some distance from the
rifles. The man immediately drew a large Arab
sword and brandishing it over his head rushed
towards me. Most providentially, as I was quite
unarmed at the time, two of his own friends put their
hands on his shoulders and held him back for a
moment. Dr. T. then endeavoured to reason with
him, and to assure him that we were men of peace
and had no desire to fight or to quarrel with him.
At this point, however, it became obvious that the
man was not alone in his hostility to us. One of his
friends struck Dr. T. a severe blow with a stick, and
immediately after two or three more drew out either
swords or daggers and advanced towards us. The
whole affair happened so quickly that when the crisis
came I had no firearm within reach, and Dr. T. had
only an unloaded and broken Winchester rifle in his

hand. A revolver shot fired by Bonner had the effect of frightening our assailants for the moment and of causing them to beat a retreat to a short distance. As, however, the effect produced was likely to be of but brief duration, and the number of people began rapidly to increase, it was obvious that we could not hope to defend ourselves in case of a renewed attack and that the only thing to be done was to beat a retreat. As soon as the position had become critical, our Hausa servants had, without an exception, run away as fast as their legs would carry them. Our Arab servant remained, shaking with fear and calling out to us to tell him in which direction he should run. Leaving our luggage beneath the trees and taking only our firearms in order to prevent them being used against us, I called out to our would-be assailants that we were going direct to the king's palace and rode off into the town. The king sent out a message to the effect that the matter should be inquired into, and assigned us a house to which we might go. Late that evening our luggage was restored to us, and on the following day our runaway servants reappeared.

As the result of what had happened, we were detained in Bida for a week, during which time the king sent a messenger down to Egga to ask the agent of the Royal Niger Company to come up and say whether we were of the same nationality as himself, or whether we were connected with the white men who had recently destroyed one of his villages. Mr. Watts, the district agent from Egga, very kindly came up for this purpose. When at length we were accorded an audience by the king, it was interesting to hear the story which he had received from our original assailant. According to his account, on our arrival in front of the town we had commenced to fire indiscriminately at a crowd of people collected there, whereupon he had heroically advanced to protect them, and waving his sword above our heads had chased us into the town. We were introduced into the king's presence by his chief minister, who is here called the "Daj." He is a venerable looking and genial old man, and speaks fluently four different languages. The king is a slight miserable-looking invalid. His palace is of immense size, and he is said to have six hundred wives resident in it. It was curious to see one of his houses covered with corrugated iron which he had obtained from the Royal Niger Company. The most interesting feature in the palace was the presence of six or eight fine ostriches which were walking up and down in his courtyard. The height of Bida, according to our calculation, is 462 feet above sea-level. The town has on the whole a much more picturesque appearance than Kano. This is chiefly due to the very large number of trees which it contains, which, especially from the north end of the town, give it the appearance of being one vast garden. A stream flows through the centre of the town, which becomes more and more difficult to ford as the rainy season advances. No attempt at a bridge has as yet been made. The houses are built in courtyards, and are similar in shape and size to those in Kano. Many of the surrounding walls have miniature roofs made of straw to keep the rain from injuring the mud. The market, though better supplied with European goods, is very much smaller than that of Kano. The population of the town has been estimated by previous visitors at from thirty to sixty thousand. The Nupé language which is spoken throughout the provinces of Bida belongs, as far as I could judge from a superficial examination of its grammar, to a totally different class of languages to Hausa. Unlike the latter, it is spoken at least as much through the nose as through the mouth.

Lying as it does within seventy miles of the River Niger, the town has frequently been visited both by European travellers and missionaries. Moreover, the agent of the Royal Niger Company, who happens to be resident at Egga, usually pays it at least an annual visit.

An average Nupé rivals, if indeed he does not actually surpass, a Hausa in the amount of cloth which he is capable of wearing about his person. His turban will take perhaps thirty yards, his pants fifteen to twenty, his tobe twenty to twenty-five, and an additional garment of some kind will not infrequently bring the total up to a hundred yards. As a large proportion of the material of which this dress is composed is imported from England, it is needless to point out how advantageous this love of extensive clothing is from the standpoint of the English manufacturer. Mr. Joseph Thomson, speaking of the ridiculous size to which the Nupé dress sometimes attains, says: "The men wear an enormous tobe, or gown, generally called an elephant tobe, from its prodigious dimensions; for, without exaggeration, there would be quite sufficient cloth in one of them to cover that quadruped." A curious characteristic of Nupé houses, which is also occasionally found in those of the Hausas, is a large clay bedstead, occupying sometimes nearly half the hut. Underneath is a hollow space where a fire is lighted in order to dry the structure and to prevent the sleeper suffering from cold. On one occasion, when lying on a bedstead of this kind, I heard several ominous cracks in the middle of the night, and found that I was rapidly descending into the fireplace beneath. Happily I had not thought fit to light the fire before retiring.

May 29.—At 3.0 this afternoon Mr. Watts and I went to salute the king for the third time and to obtain his permission to leave the town. He asked Mr. Watts for information as to the attack

which had been made by the natives of the delta
upon Akassa, and whether the Company would be
able to defend itself against its assailants. He quite
seems to imagine that the few troops to be found at
Lokoja constitute the whole English army, and, as
Mr. Watts says, the cordiality of his reception by
the king on the occasions of his visits to Bida, varies
in proportion to the number of troops which
happen to be stationed at Lokoja at that particular
time.

On leaving the king we had still to see the Daj
before actually starting. As we were engaged in
doing so, about 5.30 P.M., we were interrupted by the
arrival of another visitor who was considered of more
importance than we, and had to submit to yet
another delay. When at length this individual had
retired and we were impatiently waiting to renew
our visit, we were informed that the Daj was saying
his prayers and that we could not see him for
another half-hour. By the time our visit was concluded it was quite dark, but as we had already
been delayed six days we thought it better to make
a start rather than wait another day. By the time
that we reached the eastern gate, which was distant
from our house about a mile and a half, a most
violent rain and thunderstorm had commenced. We
were forced, therefore, to stop at the gate for the
night, where we were fortunate enough to find two

huts which afforded very tolerable shelter both to us and our goods.

May 30.—Leaving the gate of Bida this morning at 6 A.M., a two hours' march in a south-easterly direction brought us to the village of Wonangi. The country between it and Bida is open, with only an occasional patch of wood, and the soil is of a loose sandy nature. Wonangi is situated on the bank of a small stream which flows into the Niger about ten miles above Egga. In the dry season this stream is only sufficiently deep to allow of the passage of native canoes, but in the wet season it is possible for steamers drawing four or five feet and with a carrying power of two hundred tons to ascend as far as Wonangi. Here ends our long tramp from Kano. From this to England there is water communication the whole way, of which we shall, of course, avail ourselves. Despite the lack of food and other inconveniences with which we have had to put up, neither of my companions are any worse in health, if indeed they are not actually better, than when we left Kano at the end of March. As we had no further use for the donkeys, we arranged to give them to six of our servants in lieu of the wages they would otherwise have received. Our two remaining servants decided to accompany us as far as Lokoja. We engaged two canoes to carry us and our luggage, including a goat which had accompanied

S

us on our march. The larger canoe, which held most of our luggage and ourselves, was about forty or forty-five feet long and four and a half feet wide. It was made out of a single tree. Before starting the boatmen rigged up the usual covering to serve as a protection against the sun and the rain. We got away from Wonangi at 11 A.M., having first taken on board a supply of firewood and a large earthen jar in which to make a fire. Nearly all the firewood consumed in Bida is carried on men's heads from Wonangi, a distance of seven miles. It is brought to Wonangi from various points on the river bank distant in some cases as much as fifteen or twenty miles.

May 31.—At 7 P.M. yesterday evening our canoe-men grounded the boat in shallow water and passed the night thus. It rained at intervals during the night with considerable violence, and the roof of the canoe, even with the assistance of two or three sun umbrellas, entirely failed to keep us from getting wet. When it was still barely light the canoe-men pushed off, as they hoped to reach Egga before night.

The river to-day fairly realized one's ideal of what a stream in the tropics should be. It was just sufficiently narrow to show itself off to the very best advantage as seen from a canoe. We passed at times a village half hidden in the trees by the bank, and again the river would become lined with

CANOEING FROM WONANGI TO EGGA.

[To face page 258.

seemingly impenetrable forest. Every now and then a sleepy crocodile, which had been lying on the bank prior to our approach, would plunge deliberately into the water, or, if we were too far off to cause it any uneasiness, would give us a momentary glance and then resume its siesta. A little further on might be seen a hippopotamus moving slowly about in the reeds at the edge of the stream, or cooling itself in the water with nothing but its nose showing above the water. Birds of varied plumage, more especially of blue and scarlet, looked down upon us from the trees, while monkeys ran along the bank or jumped from one tree to another, chattering vigorously the while. Owing to the constant winding of the river the distance from Wonangi to Egga, which is less than seventy miles overland, is at least half as much again by water. Starting shortly before daybreak, we reached the river Niger at about three in the afternoon, and arrived at Egga at five. The Niger at the point where we joined it was about half a mile wide, and had a current of some four or five miles an hour. Its speed varies greatly from time to time according to the rainfall. Egga is situated on an island on the right bank of the Niger, and is a place of considerable importance, as although it is on the opposite side of the river to the Nupé country, it serves practically as its port. It is a most curiously pleasurable sensation to see evidence of European civilization once more in the form of a comfortable-looking English house. It is almost worth while being thoroughly uncomfortable for a time in order to enhance one's appreciation of the ordinary comforts of civilized life.

CHAPTER XIX.

EGGA TO LIVERPOOL.

IN addition to some buildings on the land, the Royal Niger Company have at Egga a large hulk anchored in the river, which serves as a sort of warehouse, and was especially built in England for this purpose. In the early days of trade on the river it was thought that Europeans living on board a hulk would be less exposed to attacks of malarial fever than those who lived on the shore; but experience seems to have shown that this is not the case, and hulks, of which at one time there were a large number on the river, are now disused, except for purposes of storing goods. During our stay at Egga two of us lived on the hulk and two on shore. On our arrival at Egga we were more than six months behindhand in our news of the outside world. It was therefore with no ordinary avidity that we set to work to absorb the contents of the pile of newspapers which were available at Egga. After spending two days here, a large portion of which was occupied in reading the papers, we re-engaged the larger of the two canoes, which had brought us down from Wonangi, to take us down to Lokoja, distant rather more than a hundred miles from Egga. The country between it and Lokoja is for the most part thinly wooded and flat, though at one or two places a range of fairly high hills approaches the river. It took us two and a half days to reach Lokoja, the canoe-men hugging one or other

CANOEING ON THE RIVER NIGER.

bank the whole way, and punting with long sticks. We arrived in time to intercept a packet of letters from England, which was about to be sent up country after us by native messenger. We were very kindly entertained at the mission-house by Lieutenant Nott, who is working on behalf of the Church Missionary Society. His companion, Mr. Watney, was seriously ill at the time of our visit,

and has, I regret to say, since died. At the time of
our arrival at Lokoja the river was lower than it had
been for very many years. Even that somewhat
mythical person, "the oldest inhabitant," failed to
recall an occasion when it had been lower. It was,
therefore, somewhat uncertain as to whether it would
be possible to go down the river to Akassa in a
steamer, or whether we should be forced to continue
our journey in a native canoe. The agent of the
Royal Niger Company having decided on the advis-
ability of attempting to send a steamer down, we
started in the ss. *Soudan* about 3 P.M. on June 7.
All went well for about ten minutes after starting,
when we had the misfortune to run on a sandbank,
and it seemed likely that we should stay there for
the night. However, owing to the energetic efforts
of our crew, who leaped into the water and eventually
succeeded in pushing the steamer off the bank, we
were able to continue our journey, and had the good
luck not to repeat our experiment. Having anchored
for the night in mid-stream, on the following day we
reached Ilushi, where we met the Swiss traveller
M. Zweifel, who is acting as a sort of traveller and
explorer for the Royal Niger Company. Despite the
adventures he has had, which would have been
sufficient to kill any three ordinary men, he seemed
to be in the very best health and spirits. On one
occasion, after losing his way in the forest, he

wandered for eight days without any other food than berries or roots, and eventually arrived at a settlement of some cannibal tribe, not a word of whose language he understood. As they stood around him, debating apparently as to when they should commence to eat him, he smiled so sweetly upon them, that they altered their mind as to the desirability of doing so, and after supplying him with food, ended by conducting him to the nearest English settlement.

On the following day, June 8, we arrived at Abutshi, a trading-station of some considerable importance. The agent here, Mr. Walker, has been thirty-two years out on the west coast, and is in perfect health. He very kindly lent me a horse, on which I rode over to Onitsha, which is the principal centre of mission work on the Niger, and is distant from Abutshi about five miles. The Church Missionary Society have here built two houses on the latest principles suggested in view of warding off malaria. In one of them four English ladies were residing, all of whom were in very good health. The mission work here is making slow but apparently genuine progress. Returning to Abutshi on the following day I found the steam-launch *Française* waiting, in which we were to continue our journey to Akassa. It had on board amongst other things six tons of ivory. Two more days brought us to Akassa at the mouth of the Niger, where we found the ss. *Accra*

engaged in taking in cargo for Liverpool. In consequence of the recent attack upon Akassa by the
natives of Brass, the Royal Niger Company were
short of their usual complement of workers, the Kroo
men being unwilling to run the chance of being eaten
by their neighbours at Brass. We had thus to wait
four days on board the *Accra* before she started on
her homeward journey. Whilst we were at Akassa,
Sir John Kirk was engaged in investigating on
behalf of the Home Government various disputes
which had arisen between the natives in the Niger
Coast Protectorate and the Royal Niger Company.
The disputes had arisen in consequence of the unwillingness of the natives to submit to the restrictions
which the Company had placed, in virtue of the
powers granted to it by its charter, on the carriage
up river of gin and modern firearms.

The following are a few final extracts from
diary :—

June 16.—Finished unloading three hundred tons
of coal. Started at 9.30 this morning. There is a
wonderful sense of freedom on the open sea after a
year spent in the interior of the Dark Continent. It
appears that in the attack which was made upon
Akassa, the Christian natives of Brass who took part
in it did so on condition that the prisoners captured
should not be eaten. After the attack the heathen
demanded that all the prisoners should be given

them to eat. The Christians, however, succeeded in rescuing twenty-six of the prisoners, and sent them down in safety to Sir Claude Macdonald, the consul-general.

June 17.—Anchored last night outside the Forcados bar, and entered the Forcados river this morning. The *Biafara*, another steamer belonging to this line, which left Akassa just ahead of us, struck this morning on the Forcados bar, and is in danger of becoming a total wreck.

June 29.—We have now been dawdling about looking for cargo for no less than twelve days. This particular spot has the reputation of being the most unhealthy spot on the whole of the west coast. The most provoking feature of the case is that even the Company gain no possible advantage by keeping us here, as they have a practical monopoly of the trade, and any cargo left by one steamer is taken on by the next. A large proportion of the passengers and crew, including the captain, are more or less seriously ill. Mark Twain speaks of a boat in which he once sailed which went so slowly, that at the end of the voyage none of the passengers could remember in what year they had started. It would almost seem as though our boat must be a descendant of this one, or that at any rate the crew of Mark Twain's ship has been transferred to ours.

June 30.—Left Forcados yesterday morning and

anchored off Lagos last night. From all accounts
this past year seems to have been the most unhealthy
ever known on this coast. During the last fifteen
months forty-six out of a hundred and fifty Europeans
resident in Lagos have died. In the Gold Coast
Colony matters have been even worse. According to
the statement of a Government official, seventy-two
out of a white population of two hundred, *i.e.*, thirty-
six per cent. have died during the previous six
months. In ordinary years about fifteen per cent.
die annually. Elmina, one of the most healthy-
looking places in the colony, has suffered the worst.

July 9.—Reached Sierra Leone at 7 P.M. last
night. Curious to say, this year has been a healthier
one than usual here, last year having been the
extreme opposite. It would almost seem as though a
pestilential wave of malaria were gradually moving
along the coast. In this case the Cameroons and the
Congo will be the greatest sufferers next year. It
has been suggested by several that the disease which
has been so prevalent in the Gold Coast Colony and
at Lagos this year is not malarial fever at all but
yellow fever. Most of the doctors, however, are
opposed to this view, yellow fever being a very rare
visitant to this coast. Moreover, the diseases are
too distinct to run one into the other at all. I
landed at Fourah Bay College, and saw Mr. Hum-
phreys and Mr. Alvarez, who had just returned from

a short journey into the interior, in the course of which they had received fifty offers from Christian natives to go into the far interior as missionaries to their heathen brethren. The Bishop of Sierra Leone is away in the West Indies at the present moment looking for native missionaries, whom he may bring over here. As the place here is garrisoned with troops brought from the West Indies, it seems natural that native missionaries should be obtained from the same source. Before leaving Sierra Leone we were informed that a telegram had just been received from England, stating that the Liberal Government had resigned, and that Lord Salisbury had again become Prime Minister. We are left to conjecture as to what has happened or what the cause of resignation has been.

July 18.—Reached Los Palmas, the capital of Grand Canary, yesterday morning. Salam, our Arab servant, will remain here until he can catch a French steamer to Marseilles, whence he can obtain one direct to Tunis.

July 23.—Passing the Welsh Coast. Hope to reach Liverpool about midnight or early to-morrow morning.

I would conclude this chapter by adding a few notes in regard to the outfit which, judging by our own experience, the traveller proposing to visit Hausaland would find most serviceable. White cotton cloth, made of really good material, we found would always obtain a ready sale. The Hausas do not seem to understand how to bleach cloth, and therefore prefer white to any other colour. If he can possibly obtain them, the traveller would do well to take a large supply of Maria Theresa dollars, which he will find no difficulty in selling at any town he may pass. As he will be expected to make presents, varying in value from a shilling to thirty pounds, to the chiefs of every town and village that he passes, it is a matter of great importance to select presents that are likely to prove acceptable. Silk goods are very generally appreciated, but these need not be of the best quality, as expensive silks will not be valued at their real worth. In addition to a large quantity of expensive silk, I took out two or three dozen silk rugs made of refuse silk and sold by Whiteley at one and elevenpence the rug. These suited the native taste exactly, and I regretted not having brought ten times the quantity. Watches and musical-boxes are not appreciated except in Kano itself. Blocks of camphor, which cost twopence each in London, will sell in Hausaland at from six to nine times this amount. Fish-hooks are in great request almost everywhere, as the hooks, which the natives make with their own iron, are very inferior to those imported from England. The traveller should be provided with an indefinite number of small presents, as no one article will ever satisfy anyone. He always expects to receive at least three or four different articles. Scissors, knives, needle-cases, pipes, scented snuff, and red Arab fezzes, we found most generally useful. Passing on to his more personal outfit, the article of most importance to the traveller is a good filter. The one which I took and which I believe to be by far the best is the Berkfield filter. It is made in several different sizes, the principle of its action being to draw the water by means of a small hand force pump through a com-posite stone of extremely fine texture. Water of a thick muddy appearance and with a most uninviting odour, if passed through this filter, will come out clear and sparkling and without a trace of its former odour. We took with us three of the stone stems supplied for the filter, but were unfortunate enough to break two of them and to wear out the other long before our journey was completed. One of these stems should be taken for every month which it is proposed to spend in travelling. We took with us sixty pounds' worth of medicines, hoping to utilize the greater part of them in doing medical work amongst the natives. We found that as a rule the more complicated medicines were of very little use, and some of these we buried before leaving Kano in order to prevent any harm resulting from their use. Simple medicines, especially pills, of which we took some fifteen thousand, we found to be greatly appreciated. Croton oil pills should be taken in large quantities, as these are perhaps more appreciated than any others. For our own use nothing could have been better than the tabloids kindly supplied by Messrs. Burroughs & Wellcome. Edginton's tents are usually recommended as the best, though we found that on more than one occasion they failed to keep out the rain. The traveller should, if possible, take some tent-pegs that the white ants cannot eat. Edginton also supplies a folding armchair called the Congo chair, which we found most serviceable. The traveller's life may sometimes depend upon the comfort of his chair, in which during an attack of fever he will sit for long hours at a time. It is impossible to carry any large supply of English food any distance up the country, but it is desirable to be provided with tea, saccharine, and arrowroot. The latter is invaluable in case of fever. We took Burroughs & Wellcome's tea tabloids, and were thoroughly satisfied with them. One thing which it is impossible to obtain in the country is good rope. If the traveller meditates employing beasts of burden of any kind he should take a very large supply of English rope.

The only scientific instruments which we took with us were, a sextant, chronometer watch, plane table for surveying, aneroids, boiling-point thermometer and pedometer. The last is of little or no use owing to the rough nature of the travelling. A plane table is also of but little use as it tends to excite the suspicion of the natives. In using a sextant it is possible to avoid this by taking one's observations at night.

CHAPTER XX.

CONCLUSION.

NOT long ago I was being shown over the House of Commons and the various buildings attached to it. On entering the map room of the House, the member who was kindly acting as my guide told me that he had recently overheard two Irish members of Parliament, who were standing in front of a wall map of South America, disputing one with another as to where Egypt was to be found on this map! Surely the time has nearly come when electors may consider themselves justified in demanding as a preliminary qualification on the part of those who seek their suffrages, an intelligent interest in those parts of the world for which we are directly or indirectly responsible. Most fortunately, in view of our future connection with the vast country of which this book treats, the initiative in asserting our influence was not left to Parliament. Had it been so there is little doubt that the half million square miles which are now secured to British influence and British trade would have passed to other hands. The question which, thanks to the efforts of private individuals,

T

has now become a possible one, still remains to be answered, What are we to do with the vast area over which we have now secured so indisputable a title ?

There are some perhaps to whom the extreme unhealthiness of the West Coast would naturally suggest the reply, that the advantage to be gained by the opening up of these regions can never be proportionate to the loss of life which it must necessarily involve. They would in fact be disposed to apply to these districts the Irishman's description of his own land, "It is a magnificent country to live out of." But there are others, and they are by no means few in number, who see in the opening up of fresh fields of trade and enterprise abroad the best solution of social difficulties at home, to whom moreover the cry for help from unnumbered millions of slaves appeals with irresistible force, and who believe that to the Anglo-Saxon race has been committed an unique opportunity for civilising and Christianising the natives of Africa. To such the difficulties or dangers above alluded to will appear of but small account compared with the magnificence of the task which it is their privilege to undertake.

The sixth International Geographical Congress, which met in London in July last, was largely occupied with the consideration of the question, To what extent is Tropical Africa suited for development by the white races or under their superintendence ?

The papers read were chiefly devoted to a discussion as to the possibility or otherwise of establishing European colonies within the limits of the tropics. The two conditions stated by Sir John Kirk and in regard to which there was a general consensus of opinion, were first that "the climate, as expressed chiefly by the diurnal and yearly range of temperature, and the moisture present in the air, must approximate to those of countries already settled by Europe," and secondly "aggravated malaria must be absent." He further stated that in order to secure these two conditions the elevation of the proposed colony must not be less than five thousand feet Even if we place the limit of elevation a thousand feet lower than Sir John Kirk suggests, it would still be the case that no part of the Hausa States or of the whole of the Central Soudan fulfils this necessary condition. When, moreover, we add to this that aggravated malaria is found with more or less frequency throughout the whole of this area, we are forced to accept the conclusion that the colonisation of Hausaland is and will ever remain impossible. By colonisation is of course implied the establishment of permanent homes and the rearing of families, as opposed to more or less prolonged visits to the country in question followed by an ultimate return to Europe. In this, the strict sense of the word, no part of Hausaland will ever be colonised from Europe. Fortunately our Empire with its never setting sun provides us with no lack of colonies in which all the conditions above stated are amply fulfilled. But if Hausaland cannot be colonised by Englishmen, it can none the less be governed and exploited by them to the mutual advantage of the governors and the governed.

Two things will have to be done before we can confer any permanent benefits upon the natives, or obtain any definite advantage for ourselves. Slave raiding must be stopped and trade communication must be improved by means of a railway. The two go together and it will be impossible fully to secure the one without the assistance afforded by the other. Happily we have in the present Secretary of State for the Colonies a man who is fully alive to the necessity of making a forward movement in regard to the development of our colonies in general, and of our possessions in West Africa in particular. In August last a deputation of persons specially interested in West Africa waited upon Mr. Chamberlain in order to press upon him the desirability of affording government assistance for the construction of three different railways on the west coast, one of which was to proceed from Lagos in the direction of the Hausa States. In illustration of the growth of trade in West Africa they pointed out that, whereas twelve years ago, there were twenty-five tons of rubber worth two thousand three hundred pounds exported, in 1890 this amount had increased to fifteen hundred tons, worth two hundred and thirty thousand pounds. They stated moreover their belief that "trade was only in its infancy in those regions, as there were no proper means of transport. Rubber cost ten pounds a ton for a carriage of fifty-five miles, and trade was suffering from being deprived of its natural hinterland." In reply to this deputation, Mr. Chamberlain made the following encouraging and significant statement. He said :—

"As to the general principle, I certainly go as far as the furthest of you . . . . it is only in such a policy of development that I can see any solution of those great social problems by which we are surrounded. Plenty of employment and a contented people go together, and there is no way of securing plenty of employment for the United Kingdom except by developing old markets and creating new ones. A distinct responsibility lies upon this country in connection with its dealings with these vast populations which come under its control. The only dominion which can compare with the British dominion is the old empire of the Romans, and it was to the credit of the Romans that wherever they went, even in barbarous countries, they left traces of their passage in admirable public works. . . . Great Britain has in many cases neglected this duty of a mother country, very much to her own injury as well as to that of the populations under her care. . . . If the people of this country are not willing to invest some of their superfluous wealth in the development of their great estate, then I see no future for these countries, and it would have been better never to have gone there."

Referring more particularly to the proposed railway from Lagos he said :—

"The Lagos railway may be said to be almost commenced. We have authorised the construction of bridges, which are the first matters to be arranged for, and we shall authorise without the slightest hesitation the completion of the railway as soon as the surveys are officially completed, and we shall endeavour in the meantime to push on these surveys as quickly as possible."*

The completion of the railway here referred to, will, I trust, be followed with the least possible delay by its continuation to the Niger as suggested in Chapter X., and eventually by its continuation to Kano and possibly Lake Tchad.

I cannot bring this chapter to a conclusion more suitably than by adopting the words of one of Africa's most distinguished explorers :—

"The question now before the civilized world is, whether the slave trade in Africa, which causes at the lowest estimate an annual loss of over half a million lives, is to be permitted to continue. Every one worthy of the name of a man will say, no! Let us then hope that England, which has hitherto occupied the proud position of being foremost amongst the friends of the unfortunate slave, may still hold that place. Let those who seek to employ money, now lying idle, join together to open the trade of Africa. Let those who desire to stamp out the traffic in slaves, put their shoulder to the wheel in earnest, and by their voice, money and energy, aid those to whom the task is entrusted. Let those interested in missionary efforts aid to their utmost those who are labouring in Africa, and send them

* Cf. *Times*, August 24th, 1895.

worthy assistants, prepared to devote their lives to the task.

"It is not by talking and writing that Africa is to be regenerated, but by action. . . . All cannot travel or become missionaries or traders, but they can give their cordial assistance to those whose duties lead them to the as yet untrodden places of the world. . . . Many a name must be added to the roll of those who have fallen in the cause of Africa; much patient and enduring labour must be gone through without flinching or repining before we see Africa truly free and happy. . . .

"Let us, therefore, work soberly and steadily, never being driven back or disheartened by any apparent failure or rebuff; but, should such be met with, search for the remedy, and then press on all the more eagerly. And so in time, with God's blessing on the work, Africa may be free and happy."*

* 'Across Africa,' by Captain Cameron, ii., p. 338.

COWRY SHELLS.

APPENDICES.

APPENDIX. I.

ITINERARIES.

Loko to Kaffi.

1st day.—*Wisherogo*, a small village of about two hundred inhabitants. Distance, 7 miles. Direction, N. Aneroid reading, 6 P.M., 29·70. Apparent height, 715 feet above sea-level. Height of Loko, 425 feet.

2nd day.—Camp, 11 miles from Wisherogo. Crossed R. Keraka half a mile after starting.

3rd day.—Camp, 22 miles farther on. During the last ten miles, a range of partially wooded and precipitous cliffs lay to the east of us. Height, 600 to 800 feet. Crossed one large stream with native bridge and three or four smaller ones. Direction due north.

4th day.—*Nassarawa.* Distance, 11 miles. Height, 560 ft. Population, 8000 to 10,000.   Just before reaching the town, we crossed a river about half a mile in width, with very rapid current, flowing E. to W.   Course to-day N.N.W. to N.

5th day.—*Laminga.* Distance, 14 miles, a large walled village. Passed smaller village of Jemagi. Country round thinly-wooded, with grass 6 to 9 feet high.

6th day.—*Kaffi.* Distance, 12 miles. Seven miles before reaching Kaffi we crossed a large river flowing W. to E., apparently the same river which we crossed S. of Nassarawa. Height, 1000 feet.   Population, 15,000 to 20,000.

[Time occupied between Loko and Kaffi 14 days.]

Kaffi to Zaria.

1st day.—*Jimbambororo.* Distance, 8½ miles. About 1½ miles after leaving Kaffi we crossed the Nassarawa river again, flowing E. to W. Course, N.

2nd day.—*Gitata.* Distance, 11½ miles. A small Pagan village situated on the slope of a hill, which rises 1500 feet above the plain.

3rd day.—*Panda.* Distance, 14 miles. On leaving Gitata the path descended abruptly 150 feet. Crossed five streams of considerable size. One 2 miles south of Panda 110 yards wide, flowing E. to W. Height of Panda, 2170 feet.

4th day.—Camp near the village of Kukui. Distance, 7 miles. Passed to-day two large sugar-loaf hills, one 800 and the other 1200 feet above the path.

5th day.—*Arbi.* Distance, 11 miles. Height, 2225 feet. Course during last three days uniformly N.

6th day.—Camp just beyond River Zurara, 80 yards wide, flowing E. to W. Distance, 13 miles.

7th day.—*Katchia.* Distance, 17 miles. Height, 2442 feet. Population, about 7000.

8th day.—*Katill.* Distance, 15 miles. Height, 2530 feet. This is the highest place between Loko and Kano.

9th day.—*Agwura.* Distance, 16½ miles. Camp on a large granite rock just beyond the village. Five miles after leaving Katill passed small village called Adimanzauri, with a stream beyond which bears the same name. Height of camp, 2185 feet.

10th day.—*Kulla.* Distance, 11½ miles. Height, 2145 feet. Course varying from N.W. to W.

11th day.—*Gierko.* The first genuinely Hausa town. Distance, 8½ miles. Height, 1970 feet. The town is situated just beyond the River Koduna, which at the point we crossed it was flowing S.S.E. to N.N.W. It was about 400 yards wide. Soon after the point at which we crossed it turns S.S.E., and passing a little to the N. of Bida, enters the Niger about 30 miles above

Egga. Loaded canoes can ascend as far as Gierko during three or four months of the year.

12th day.—*Rikoka,* pronounced by some Likoka. Distance, 14 miles. Height, the same as Gierko. Course to-day, N.W. Passed a village called Ribako 7¼ miles after leaving Gierko.

13th day.—*Iggabi.* Distance, 3½ miles. Half a mile after leaving Rikoka crossed a deep and rapidly-flowing river called Shika. Width, 80 yards. At the point at which we crossed it was flowing W.N.W.

14th day.—*Zaria.* Distance, 17 miles. Height, according to boiling-point thermometer, 2072 feet (according to aneroid, 2080 feet). Population, 30,000. Course to-day, N. Seven miles before reaching Zaria we passed on our right a large village called Garimbautshi.

[Time occupied between Kaffi and Zaria 19 days.]

Zaria to Kano.

1st day.—*Likoro.* Distance, 10½ miles. Course, varying from N. to N.W. Crossed three small streams flowing W. to E.

2nd day.—*Kwatakori.* Distance, 8 miles. Five miles after leaving Likoro passed village of Dandabusa. Course, N. to N.N.E.

3rd day.—*Antchou.* Distance, 13½ miles. Six and a half miles after leaving Kwatakori passed village of Gimmi. Course, N.N.E. Height, 2150 feet.

4th day.—*Danzuchia.* Distance, 13 miles. Height, 1880 feet. Four miles after leaving Antchou passed large village called Allagabba. Course, N.E.

5th day.—*Yako.* Distance, 10½ miles. After going about 4 miles passed village called Kirana, and 4 miles farther on again another called Kogo.

6th day.—*Madubi.* Distance, 12 miles. Height, 1610 feet.

7th day.—*Kaffi.* Distance, 7 miles. Course, N.E. Country, flat and sandy.

8th day.—*Kano.* Distance, 10 miles. Height, 1692 feet. Longitude, 8° 29″ 15′ E. Crossed the River Mallam about halfway between Kaffi and Kano. Width of water, 60 yards, though bed of stream much wider. Course of river, from W. to E. [Time occupied between Zaria and Kano 8 days.]

Kano to Sansanni.

1st day.—Camp by the side of a small stream 7 miles S.W. of Kano.

2nd day.—*Durung.* Distance, 15 miles. A half-deserted village. Six miles before reaching it passed village called Yelwa on our right. Course, W.S.W.

3rd day.—*Kabbo.* Distance, 7 miles. Camped a mile beyond the village. Course, S.W. Height, 1830 feet.

4th day.—*Karaii.* Distance, 15 miles. Population, 5000 or 6000. Camp, ¾ mile beyond the town.

5th day.—*Dunzo.* Distance, 10 miles. Course, S.S.W.

6th day.—*Rogo.* Distance, 10 miles. Population, about 7000. Rain fell here to-day (April 15), the first since October 25.

7th day.—*Gwonggwong.* Distance, 9 miles. Course, due S. Gwonggwong is situated within the territory of Kano, but close to the borders of Katsena and Zaria.

8th day.—*Dabébé.* Distance, 12 miles. Course, S.W.

9th day.—*Denja.* Distance, 4 miles. Course, from W. to W.N.W. A mile before reaching Denja crossed a large stream called Baragoungouni.

10th day.—*Maska.* Distance, 19 miles. On leaving Denja we marched 10 miles in S.W. direction to Giwa. We then turned W., and went 9 miles to Maska. A more direct route W.S.W. from Denja passes village of Tanduma.

11th day.—*Kaia.* Distance, 10 miles. Town half deserted. Camped a mile beyond it. Course, S.S.W.

12th day.—*Idesu.* Seven and a half miles. Ruined town. Course, S. to S.S.W.

13th day.—Camp. Distance, 12 miles. Near site of large ruined town. Course, S.S.W.

14th day.—*Zogendowa.* Ruined town. Distance, 10½ miles. Course, varying from W. to W.S.W.

15th day.—*Kazeggi.* Distance, 12 miles. Crossed several deep but waterless gullies. Course, W.S.W.

16th day.—*Sansanni.* The camp of the King of Kwontagora, 6 miles beyond Birnin Gwari, which he has recently destroyed. Distance, 25 miles. Birnin Gwari, formerly a very large and important town, built on the slope of a steep hill. Course, from W. to W.S.W.

[Time actually occupied beyond Kano and Sansanni 29 days.]

Sansanni to Egga.

1st day.—Camp, a little short of a ruined village called *Kiranku.* Distance, 22 miles. Course, S. for the first 10 miles, then S.S.W. to S.W.

2nd day.—*Bugaii.* Distance, 16 miles. Direction, S.S.W. A semi-deserted town. Country hilly, intercepted by very deep gullies.

3rd day.—*Wurin Kenkina.* Half-ruined town. Distance, 15 miles. Course, W.S.W. Country much less hilly.

4th day.—*Dawakin Bassa.* Distance, 9 miles. Direction, S.S.W.

5th day.—*Nassarawa.* Distance, 6 miles. The third town of this name which we have passed.

6th day.—*Ikusu.* Distance, 13 miles. Eight miles after leaving Nassarawa we passed a village perched on a high rock named Rukoki. Course, S. for the first 9 miles, then S.S.W. Shade temperature, 96° Fahr.; this has been the average temperature for a considerable time past.

7th day.—*Karamin Unqua.* Distance, 20 miles. No water between this and Ikusu (May). Course, S.S.W. to S.W.

8th day.—*Ougou.* Distance, 16½ miles. Camped in a ravine ¾ mile beyond the town. Four miles before reaching Ougou passed large village called Teggina. Course, S.S.W. Height of Ougou, 950 feet.

9th day.—*Goumna.* Distance, 7 miles. Camped ¾ mile beyond the town. Course, S. by E.

10th day.—*Jangaro.* Distance, 16 miles. Eight miles before reaching it we passed a little to the S. of Garin Gubbats. Course for first 8 miles, W.S.W., afterwards, S.W.

11th day.—*Wushishi.* Distance, 7½ miles. Just before reaching it we crossed the River Koduna, bed ½ mile wide, stream 250 yards wide. River flowing N.E. to S.W. Course to-day, S.

12th day.—*Koramin Ayaba.* Distance, 12 miles. Course, varying from S. to S. by E. Country flat, closely wooded.

13th day.—Camp near *Baban Zauri,* a scattered place including several distinct hamlets. Distance, 6 miles. Course, S.

14th day.—*Lemo.* A large scattered village. Distance, 11 miles. Course, S.W. The first place within the territory of Bida.

15th day.—Camp, between Massalachi and Kedania. Distance, 9 miles. Course, S.S.W.

16th day.—*Bida.* Distance, 15 miles. Course, W.S.W. Population about 60,000. Height, 462 feet.

17th day.—Bank of river. A mile after leaving Bida we reached Wonangi, a village on the bank of a small stream flowing into the Niger 10 miles above Egga. During the wet season steam-launches can ascend as far as Wonangi. Course between Bida and Wonangi, S.E. Distance from Wonangi to Egga by water, about 110 miles.

18th day.—*Egga.* An important trading centre of the R. N. Co. Distance from Lokoja, 100 miles.

[Time occupied between Sansanni and Egga 30 days.]

APPENDIX II.

APPENDIX II.

THE HAUSA ASSOCIATION.

For Promoting the Study of the Hausa Language and People.

Founded in Memory of the Rev. John Alfred Robinson, M.A., late Scholar of Christ's College, Cambridge, who died at his work in the employment of the Church Missionary Society, at Lokoja, Niger Territories, on the 25th June, 1891.

General Committee.

His Grace the Archbishop of Canterbury.
His Grace the Archbishop of Dublin.
His Grace The Duke of Westminster, K.G.
The Rt. Hon. The Earl of Scarborough.
The Rt. Hon. Viscount Wolseley, K.P., &c., Field Marshal, Commander-in-Chief.
The Bishop of Salisbury.
The Bishop of Wakefield.
The Bishop of Dover.
The Bishop of Sierra Leone.
The Rt. Hon. Lord Loch, G.C.B., G.C.M.G.
The Rt. Hon. Lord Lamington, K.C.M.G., Governor of Queensland.
Sir John Kennaway, Bart., M.P., President of the Church Missionary Society.
Sir George Taubman-Goldie, K.C.M.G., Governor of the Royal Niger Company.
Sir Albert Rollit, D.C.L., M.P., President of the London Chamber of Commerce.
Sir John Kirk, G.C.M.G., K.C.B.

Col. Sir Francis Scott, K.C.M.G., C.B., Inspect.-Gen. of the Gold Coast Constabulary.*

Rev. A. J. Mason, D.D., Canon of Canterbury, Lady Margaret Professor of Divinity, Cambridge.

Rev. J. Armitage Robinson, B.D., Norrisian Professor of Divinity, Cambridge.

Rev. J. O. F. Murray, M.A., Fellow and Dean of Emmanue College, Cambridge.

Rev. Arthur W. Robinson, M.A., Vicar of All Hallows', Barking, E.C.

Rev. Wm. Allan, D.D., Bungay, Suffolk.

F. Max Müller, M.A., Professor of Comparative Philology, Oxford.

John Peile, Litt. D., Master of Christ's College, Cambridge.

D. S. Margoliouth, M.A., Professor of Arabic, Oxford.

Francis Galton, F.R.S., D.C.L., Hon. Sc.D.

Clements R. Markham, C.B., F.R.S., President of the Royal Geographical Society.

Major Leonard Darwin, R.E., F.R.S.

Captain F. D. Lugard, C.B., D.S.O.

Henry Morris, C.M.S., and British and Foreign Bible Society.

Executive Committee.

Sir G. Goldie, *Chairman.*

The Bishop of Dover, *Vice-Chairman.*

Rev. J. O. Murray, *Hon. Sec.*

Rev. Canon Mason.

Rev. A. W. Robinson.

Major Darwin.

Mr. F. Galton.

Mr. H. Morris.

Financial Committee.

Rev. J. O. F. Murray ; Mr. C. E. Malan ;
Mrs. J. M. Sinclair, *Hon. Sec.*

Hon. Treasurer.—J. H. Tritton, Esq., Messrs. Barclay, Bevan & Co., 54, Lombard Street, E.C.

* In command of the present Ashanti expedition.

The following Societies have expressed their sympathy with the objects of the Association :—

> The Royal Geographical Society.
> The Scottish Geographical Society.
> The Manchester Geographical Society.
> The Anthropological Institute.
> The Anti-Slavery Society.
> The British and Foreign Bible Society.
> The Church Missionary Society.
> The Society for the Propagation of the Gospel.

The object of the Association.

The aim of the Association is to carry on the work begun by the Rev. John Alfred Robinson, by providing for a scholarly and scientific study of the Hausa Language, with a view of promoting the higher interests of that people, and of translating the Scriptures and other appropriate literature into their tongue.

To explain the importance of their aim, something must be said about

> (1) The Hausa tongue and people.
> (2) Mr. J. A. Robinson's work and conclusions.

The Hausa tongue and people.

Hausa is the *lingua franca* of the Central Soudan, extending from the Sahara to the Pagan tribes near the Gulf of Guinea, and from the Egyptian Soudan to the French colony of Senegal. The greater portion of this region has lately been secured to British influence by treaties and international agreements. It is estimated that not less than fifteen millions of persons speak the Hausa tongue, and many of these can read and write it in a modified form of Arabic character. The importance of the Hausa language was fully appreciated forty years ago by the traveller, Dr. Barth, who endeavoured to promote its study, but with only partial success. The Central Soudan having been until lately isolated from European intercourse, the materials necessary for the accurate study of Hausa do not exist in Europe. A grammar, a dictionary, and a reading book were compiled some years ago by a German student, Dr. Schön. So important were these early efforts considered to be, that the University of Oxford granted him their honorary degree in recognition of them. A grammar and vocabulary in French has lately been brought out in Algeria. Portions of the Scriptures have also been translated into Hausa. But these being all first efforts, call for improvement. The book which best gives the idioms of the vernacular is the ' Magana Hausa,' which was taken down, for the most part, from the dictation of a native. The Hausa language is rich in words, and presents a special interest to philologists on the open question of its alleged connection with the Semitic group. The Central Soudan States possess a certain civilisation of their own, which can hardly be interpreted aright, except by those who are familiar with the prevalent language, which is Hausa. The dominant races are remarkably intelligent, but as the social system in the Central Soudan is chiefly based upon slavery, the great mass of the population exists in a condition of ignorance and insecurity which forms a striking contrast with the well-being of the slave-owning classes. The internal commerce of these regions is mainly carried on by the Hausa race proper, whose caravans travel northward to the Mediterranean, eastward to the Red Sea, southward to the Gulf of Guinea, and westward to the Atlantic. They would thus be powerful agents for disseminating over vast regions and amongst dense populations whatever ideas Europeans may succeed in planting amongst them. These Hausa traders are courteous in manner; they profess the Moslem religion, which has been outwardly imposed on the Central Soudan by the conquering races, but they are free from bigotry and open to argument. In pursuing the study of their language scientifically while in touch with the natives, it is evident that many facts of anthropological, demographic, and other interest will come to light.

U

Mr. J. A. Robinson's Work and Conclusions.

Mr. J. A. Robinson's missionary work on the Niger dates from 1886, but, during the last two years of his life, he devoted his attention mainly to the Central Soudan. Having acquired the Hausa language, he lived among the people in a manner calculated to disarm suspicion and promote good understanding by close and friendly intercourse, and successfully demonstrated that much could be effected on the lines which he had laid down. Before his death he had concluded a careful revision in Hausa of the early chapters of the Gospel according to St. Matthew, and he has left various notes and materials which will doubtless be of value to future students. His experience convinced him, first, that no satisfactory work of any kind could be carried on amongst these races without careful study of Hausa, in order to ascertain their modes of thought, and communicate European ideas to them without fear of misunderstanding; secondly, that, in respect of mission work, the most effective method would be to place within their reach an accurate translation of the Scriptures into their own tongue; and thirdly, that this initial work, important as it is, would be incomplete unless it were given continuity and growth by providing instruction to students, and thus gradually disseminating a knowledge of the Hausa language amongst the Europeans who may henceforth visit those regions. for missionary, administrative, or commercial objects.

Results achieved.

To promote the objects of the Association, the Executive Committee decided to appoint a "Robinson Student" to study the language and customs of the Hausas, and to gather materials for the translation of the Scriptures.

After the careful consideration of numerous applications in answer to advertisements inserted in leading Scientific, Literary, and Religious periodicals, they determined to invite one of Mr. Robinson's brothers, the Rev. Charles H. Robinson, M.A.— a man of academic distinction, varied experience, and tried capacity in Oriental travel—to be the first "Student" of the Association.

The next step was to despatch him to Tripoli and Tunis, where extensive Hausa colonies exist, so that he might carry on his preliminary studies in as healthy a region as possible.

The result of this stay in North Africa included the publication in the Hausa character of a careful revision of John Alfred Robinson's translation of St. Matthew, and a paper before the British Association, published in the Journal of the Royal Geographical Society for November, 1893.

The third step was for Mr. Robinson, who had associated with himself a qualified medical man, Dr. Tonkin, and an assistant, Mr. Bonner, to proceed with his companions by way of the Rivers Niger and Benué to Loko, and thence by a difficult and toilsome overland journey of about 350 miles to Kano, the commercial centre of Hausaland, and while probably the most populous, certainly the most important town of all tropical Africa.

Mr. Robinson on his return journey followed a different route, some 425 miles overland, part of which had never before been traversed by any European, and leading from Kano to Egga on the Niger. He and his companions arrived safely in England on July 24th, 1895.

He has brought back with him (1) a careful revision of Dr. Schön's dictionary, augmented by at least 3000 words; (2) materials for an adequate grammar of the Hausa language; (3) a collection of native MSS., consisting of history and of historical and religious songs, translated into English and ready for publication; (4) idiomatic translations of the Gospels of St. Luke and St. John.

Dr. Tonkin has been able to make a number of scientific observations, which will be communicated to the proper Societies.

The funds of the Society are exhausted, and it is estimated that a sum of £1000 is still required for the adequate publication of the materials collected.

'Occasional Papers' (price 1*d.* each, or 6*d.* a dozen), were issued from time to time by Mr. Robinson, describing his work in Africa and reporting the progress made. They are still to be obtained from Mrs. J. M. Sinclair, Bonny Glen, Donegal, to whom also subscriptions may be paid.

Messrs. Sampson Low, Marston & Co. will publish in January, 1896, a work by Mr. Robinson, entitled 'Hausaland.'

It is further hoped that the result of a public appeal for funds may enable some permanent Institution to be founded for the continuous diffusion of knowledge of this Hausa language, so little known, though spoken by over one hundredth of the whole human race, and of this Hausa people, for whose civilisation Great Britain has now accepted the moral responsibility.

GEORGE TAUBMAN-GOLDIE, *Chairman.*
JOHN OWEN MURRAY, *Hon. Sec.*

Messrs. Barclay, Bevan, Tritton & Co. have accepted the account of the Association, and Subscriptions or Donations may be sent to them at 54, Lombard Street, London, E.C., to be placed to the credit of the Hausa Association.

APPENDIX III.

TOTEMISM.

The superstition referred to (p. 36) is obviously connected with the totemism which is found amongst almost all savages. A totem has been defined as "a class of material objects which a savage regards with superstitious respect, believing that there exists between him and every member of the class, an intimate and altogether special relation. The name is derived from an Ojibway word totem.... Considered in relation to man, totems are of at least three kinds: (1) the clan totem, common to a whole clan, and passing by inheritance from generation to generation; (2) the sex totem, common either to all the males or to all the females of a tribe, to the exclusion in either case of the other sex; (3) the individual totem, belonging to a single individual and not passing to his descendants." The totemism referred to on the Niger, belongs apparently to this third class. Mr. J. G. Frazer, in his work on Totemism, gives several instances as occurring in South Australia, almost exactly similar to the one narrated above. In regard to the geographical spread of totemism, it is found generally in North America, except amongst the Esquimaux. In South America it is found in Venezuela, Guiana, and Patagonia. In Africa it is found in several portions of Central Africa, both on the East and the West coast, also amongst the Damaras and the Bechuanas of the south. Traces of it apparently exist in Abyssinia and Madagascar. In Bengal it is found amongst the non-Aryan tribes. It is also apparently found in Siberia and China. In Australia it is practically universal. It has been found also in Samoa, and in several of the islands of Melanesia. The taboos which are placed on particular plants and trees by the chiefs in the Niger delta, are perhaps to be connected with totemism.

The only possible trace of totemism which I was able to discover amongst the Hausas themselves, was the possession by individuals of names denoting various animals. No idea of totemism is apparently connected with the possession of such names now, but it is possible that it may have been so originally.

APPENDIX IV.

The following is a list of the books published on the Hausa people or language during the last half century :—

'Travels and discoveries in North and Central Africa,' 1849–1855 by *Dr. Barth.* Published in five volumes in 1857, and republished in two small vols. in 1890. Dr. Barth, who was a native of Germany, went out as assistant to Mr. Richardson, who was sent by the British Government to explore the countries lying to the south of the Sahara, and on the death of Mr. Richardson, he took charge of the expedition, and carried it to a successful issue. Though written in rather an uninteresting style, these volumes contain a vast amount of information, not only in regard to the Hausas, but in regard to several other races inhabiting the Central Soudan. Dr. Barth was one of the first to give a full account of the town of Timbuktu.

In addition to the above, Dr. Barth published in 1862, at Gotha, 'Sammlung und Bearbeitung Central-Afrikanischer Vokabularien,' specimens of, and remarks upon, some ten or twelve African languages including Hausa.

Dr. J. F. Schön, also of German nationality, though he was never able to visit any part of the Hausa country, spent many years in the study of this language, and published several works on it, including a dictionary, a grammar, and some Hausa stories taken down by dictation from a native in England. These last, which are published by the Society for Promoting Christian Knowledge, under the title of ' Magana Hausa,' afford by far the best material at present available for the study of Hausa in England. The dictionary has for some time past been out of print. Dr. Schön also published translations of several portions of the Bible in Hausa, but these being written in English characters, and being in very un-idiomatic Hausa, will require a large amount of revision and correction before they can be of any use.

Dr. W. B. Baikie, who was for many years English Consul at Lokoja, collected some materials for the study of the Hausa language, which, however, have never been published. The only account of his work published, is to be found in the Journal of the Royal Geographical Society, vol. 37, pp. 92–108, entitled ' Notes of a Journey from Bida in Nupe, to Gano in Haussa, performed in 1862, extracted from portions of Dr. Baikie's journals in the possession of the Foreign Office, by J. Kirk, M.D.' Unfortunately, the notes which Dr. Baikie is supposed to have made in regard to the town of Kano have been lost. The published notes contain very little information in regard to the country or the people, but consist chiefly of details of travel.

Mr. Joseph Thompson published in ' Good Words,' 1886, a very brief account of his journey, during the previous year, to Sokoto and back.

A work entitled ' Essai de dictionnaire de la langue Haoussa, par *M. le Roux,*' was published in Algiers in 1886. This, however, consists almost as much of Arabic as of Hausa words, the author being apparently completely ignorant of either language.

'Saint Louis à Tripoli par le Tchad,' published by *Colonel Monteuil* in 1894, gives an account of the author's travels from Senegambia to Lake Tchad, *viâ* Kano, and thence across the Sahara to Tripoli. This book contains an interesting description of the town of Kano, but very little information in regard to the Hausa people, and none in regard to the language, which the author had not himself studied.

'Im Herzen der Haussa-lander, von *Paul Staudinger,*' published in Leipzig in 1891, contains an account of a journey made by the author through a considerable portion of the Hausa States, including a visit to Kano and Sokoto.

I may perhaps conclude this list by stating that the Cambridge University Press will shortly publish the Hausa manuscripts which I brought back with me, reproduced in facsimile, together with translations and notes.

INDEX.

LONDON: PRINTED BY WILLIAM CLOWES AND SONS, LIMITED,
STAMFORD STREET AND CHARING CROSS.

751503

Made in the USA